I'm Sur
Methodists...

*Diary of
John H.W. Stuckenberg
Chaplain of the
145th Pennsylvania
Volunteer Infantry*

David T. Hedrick
&
Gordon Barry Davis Jr.

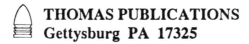
THOMAS PUBLICATIONS
Gettysburg PA 17325

Copyright © 1995 David T. Hedrick and Gordon Barry Davis, Jr.

Printed and bound in the United States of America

Published by THOMAS PUBLICATIONS, P.O. Box 3031, Gettysburg, Pa. 17325

All rights reserved. No part of this book may be used or reproduced without written permission of the author and the publisher, except in the case of brief quotations embodied in critical essays and reviews.

ISBN-0-939631-75-X

Cover design by Ryan C. Stouch

Cover illustration "Gettysburg Battlefield Series No. 11" by George Leo Frankenstein courtesy of Gettysburg College.

Photo Credits

Erie Museum and Planetarium: 49
Frank Leslie's Illustrated History of the Civil War: 39, 73
Gannon University Historical Museum: 70
Gettysburg College: 2, 22, 23, 114
Irwin Rider Collection: 15, 35
Library of Congress photo, courtesy of William A. Frassanito: 13, 40, 86
Luther Memorial Church: 4, 67
Miller Family: 45, 85
Peter C. Vermilyea: 97
U.S. Army Miliary History Institute (USAMHI): 61, 65
USAMHI photo, courtesy of William A. Frassanito: 54

TABLE OF CONTENTS

	Introduction 1	
Chapter 1	Introduction to Army Life	
	September 11 - October 27, 1862 11	
Chapter 2	Moving South to Fredericksburg	
	October 28 - December 9, 1862 27	
Chapter 3	Fredericksburg Battle	
	December 10 - 16, 1862 37	
Chapter 4	Christmas Leave	
	December 17, 1862 - February 22, 1863 47	
Chapter 5	Winter Camp and Chancellorsville	
	March - May 9, 1863 56	
Chapter 6	Chasing the Army of Northern Virginia	
	May 12 - July 1, 1863 68	
Chapter 7	Gettysburg	
	July 2 - 6, 1863 77	
Chapter 8	Return to Virginia	
	July 7 - 28, 1863 88	
Chapter 9	Post Battle Stress	
	July 29 - September 10, 1863 100	
Appendix 1	From the Lutheran Observer of March 6, 1863 115	
Appendix 2	Prayer for a Day of National Humiliation, Fasting,	
	and Prayer, April 30, 1863 117	
	Notes 119	
	Bibliography 135	
	Index 139	

List of Illustrations

Chaplain John Henry Wilburn Stuckenberg 2
J.H.W. Stuckenberg later in life 4
A Union burial detail at Antietam 13
Colonel Hiram L. Brown 15
Members of the Regimental Church, October 5, 1862 22
Second Lieutenant George A. Evans, Company I 35
"A street in Fredericksburg, VA...." 39
Caroline Street, Fredericksburg 40
Map of the battle of Fredericksburg 42
Captain Charles M. Lynch, Company D 45
Private Robert W. Finn, Company D 49
Mary Washington's monument 54
Chancellor House 61
Map of the battle of Chancellorsville 63
Lieutenant Colonel David B. McCreary 65
The First English Evangelical Lutheran Church, Erie 67
Captain John W. Reynolds 70
"Thoroughfare Gap, Va...." 73
Map of the battle of Gettysburg 82
Lieutenant Horatio F. Lewis, Company D 85
Confederate dead gathered for burial 86
Monument to the 145th Pa. Inf. at Gettysburg 87
Thoroughfare Gap, 1993 97
Chaplain John Stuckenberg 114

INTRODUCTION

Chaplain Stuckenberg

John Henry Wilburn Stuckenberg, chaplain of the 145th Pennsylvania Volunteers from September 1862 to October 1863, was born January 6, 1835, in Bramasche, Germany. Emigrating with his family in 1839, he grew up in western Pennsylvania, southern Ohio, and southern Indiana. Entering Wittenburg College in 1852, he received his B.A. degree in 1857, and remained at this young Lutheran institution for one year of theological study. Upon completion of his advanced study in 1858, he accepted an appointment as pastor to a struggling Lutheran congregation in Davenport, Iowa. By the end of one year in Iowa, Stuckenberg recognized his need for more formal study. In 1859 he returned to Germany for two additional years of theological study at the University of Halle.

Pastor Stuckenberg departed from Europe in the summer of 1861. Upon his return to the United States he accepted a pastoral call to three churches in the Erie, Pennsylvania, area. The next year saw his congregations grow, his relations with members of other denominations cordially solidified, and his place as a promising young pastor in a growing community assured.

During a vacation after his first year as a pastor, Wilburn wrote his brother, Herman, in Cincinnati: "You will confer quite a favor on me, if, in case we are not exempt, you have my name enrolled among the militia. I despise the mean attempts made to shirk duties to our country at present; and if I am drafted my course of duty will be plain."[1] On September 10, 1862 he applied for the chaplaincy of the third regiment to be raised from northwestern Pennsylvania. His Civil War diary commences October 6, 1862 and concludes on September 10, 1863.

The diary that Chaplain Stuckenberg began shortly after his entry into the military consists of 134 pages in two parts. The first section is written on pre-folded 11 1/8" x 15 7/8" lined paper and is stitched together in a single gathering. The second segment is written on 9 7/8" x 15 7/8" lined paper and is sewn in five gatherings. It is written entirely in ink. In using the diary in his 1938 biography, *The Life of J.H.W. Stuckenberg*, John O. Evjen added numerous blue and red pencil marks to many pages.

Some of Stuckenberg's entries were written days or weeks after the events being described [eg. chapters 4 and 5] while other entries were written within minutes of the events described [eg. October 27, 1862, and entries in August 1863]. There were no diary entries written between December 10, 1862, and March 24, 1863. However, two other manuscripts, from that period, written by Stuckenberg have been incorporated into this narrative. Again from May 9 through July 29 there are no dated diary entries.

Upon his return to his pastorate in the fall of 1863, Stuckenberg resumed the life of a Lutheran parish pastor and continued his extremely active involvement in Erie. By 1865 he decided once again to pursue graduate study in Germany, spending one

Chaplain John Henry Wilburn Stuckenberg

semester each at the Universities at Gottingen, Berlin, and Tubingen. He returned to the United States in 1866 serving this time as a parish pastor first in Indianapolis and later in Pittsburgh. On October 27, 1869, Stuckenberg married Mary Gingrich, the daughter of a good friend and mentor from Erie; he had proposed—more than three years earlier—just before leaving on his second trip to Germany.

From 1873 to 1880 Wilburn was a member of the faculty at Wittenburg College; from 1880 to 1895 he lived and worked in Germany, and commencing in 1896 he once again resided in the United States. Throughout his life Stuckenberg wrote an impressive number of articles for both popular and scholarly publications, and it was during this period that his intellectual effort was most evident.[2] His most important books included: *Christian Sociology*, 1880; *Life of Immanual Kant*, 1882; *Introduction to the Study of Philosophy*, 1888 (four additional printings), 2nd edition 1896 (three additional printings); and *The Final Science or Spiritual Materialism*, 1885, *The Social Problem*, 1897; *Introduction to the Study of Sociology*, 1897 (three additional editions); and *Sociology the Science of Human Society*, 1903.

In 1903 the Stuckenbergs traveled to Europe—he to conduct research in London's libraries, she to attend temperance conventions in Bremen and Geneva. John died quite suddenly on May 28, 1903. After memorial services in England, Mary had the body cremated prior to her return to the United States.

Mary Stuckenberg spent much of the rest of her life in Gettysburg. She remained an activist for temperance and women's rights, and is best known in Gettysburg as the founder of the Woman's League of Gettysburg College. Mary died in 1934, and both she and John are buried in the Gettysburg National Cemetery. Their gravestone reads: "Now we see through a glass darkly—but we see."

J. H. W. Stuckenberg has been all but been ignored by 20th century scholars. His biography of Kant was the first in the English Language, and his *Christian Sociology* was written twenty years before the Social Gospel movement swept America. In the words of Dr. Richard Hoehn, one of the few scholars to study Stuckenberg in this century: "Lutheran histories describe him as 'a real prophet of social Christianity' in his early years, but then as having drifted away from the Lutheran Church in America and from the Christian grounds for social action."[3] Hoehn, on the other hand, feels that: "Stuckenberg never became less Lutheran, though he did become more German-Lutheran than American-Lutheran, and more scholarly than pastoral. He was a liberal. From his perspective it was the American Church, not he, that had drifted away from the great principles of the Reformation."[4] Stuckenberg made his position very clear in his 'Last Will and Testament' dated 6 June 1898: "I favor a progressive Christianity based on the living teachings of Christ and his Apostles. I am opposed to the Stagnation created by religious dogmatism and traditionalism, and wish none of my possessions to be used in the interest of this stagnation."[5]

Civil War scholars have not discovered Stuckenberg—most likely because there is no published history of his regiment. His diary was used quite heavily in a biography, *The Life of J.H.W. Stuckenberg* by John O. Evjen, published in 1938. A single very brief chapter is devoted to his Civil War experiences. One of the most recent scholars to study Civil War Chaplains did not mention Stuckenberg, and his study contains almost nothing of the contributions of Lutherans who served as Civil War Chaplains.[6] An exhaustive literature search conducted by Richard Hoehn in preparation for the publication of *Now We See Through A Glass Darkly—But We See: The Papers of J. H. W. and Mary G. Stuckenberg* (Gettysburg College, 1987) did not uncover any new articles related to the Civil War period.

J.H.W. Stuckenberg later in life.

The 145th Pennsylvania Infantry

The 145th Pennsylvania Volunteers must be considered one of the real hard luck regiments of the Civil War. This third regiment raised in the northwest corner of Pennsylvania was under the shadow of both the 83rd Pennsylvania Volunteers with its local hero, Colonel Strong Vincent, and the 111th Pennsylvania Volunteers.

The invasion of Maryland in August 1862, had provided the catalyst for the creation of the 145th Pennsylvania Volunteers. Nine of the regiment's ten companies filled their ranks and were mustered into federal service on September 5, 1862. Company K completed its recruiting shortly thereafter and was mustered in on September 12. The officers elected by the regiment were all well known in northwestern Pennsylvania: Hiram L. Brown, an Erie hotel keeper and veteran of the 83rd Pennsylvania Volunteers was selected as Colonel; David B. McCreary, a lawyer and educator became the regiment's Lieutenant-Colonel; the unit's Major was John W. Patton, the publisher/editor of the Conneautville Courier and a leading figure in Crawford County Republican politics.[7]

The need for troops at the front was so great that Governor Andrew Curtin ordered the regiment to the front on September 10, 1862, and without delay the regiment departed Erie on September 11; (Company K and Chaplain Stuckenberg's departure was delayed until September 15). As the order was unexpected, the unit departed Erie lacking both weapons and equipment. After a 36 hour ride via Buffalo, Elmira, and Harrisburg, the regiment arrived at Chambersburg, Pennsylvania, on September 13th. Old 69 caliber Harpers Ferry muskets and leather accouterments were issued to the new troops, but tents and other equipment were still unavailable. On September 17 the unit was ordered to picket duty on the Chesapeake and Ohio Canal, and shortly thereafter found themselves with the thankless but necessary task of burying the dead from Antietam.

At the end of September the 145th rejoined the Army of the Potomac in camp near Harpers Ferry. While at that location the regiment was temporarily assigned to the famous Irish Brigade, an arrangement not pleasing to the feisty Irishmen nor to the untrained, prudish, and prejudiced rookies. Illness ravaged the ranks, and at one point during the fall of 1862, more that half the men were on sick leave.

November 1862 found the 145th encamped on Stafford Heights opposite the old colonial city of Fredericksburg. On December 13, eight companies of the 145th were engaged in the battle for Mayre's Heights. At the end of the day the unit had lost 34 men killed, 152 wounded, and an additional 43 listed as missing. Despite the losses, the unit was publicly rebuked by General Caldwell: "The regiments, however, all behaved with the greatest gallantry and fought with steadiness, except the One hundred and forty-fifth Pennsylvania, which broke and fell back, its colonel being severely wounded."[8]

By the spring of 1863 the regiment was ready to redeem itself, but again the fortunes of war would not favor the men of the 145th. Portions of the regiment and other units from the First Brigade who had been assigned picket duty near Chancellorsville failed to receive an order to withdraw. Lieutenant Colonel McCreary, 5 line officers, and 116 men were captured. The unit's bravery was once again questioned.

Moving North in June 1863 the regiment was last in the Second Corps' line of march, and arrived at Gettysburg late on the evening of July 1. But this time there can be no question of the unit's valor. Engaged in the Wheatfield and nearby woods, the 145th had the dubious honor of holding the most advanced position of their brigade. At Gettysburg the regiment entered the field with slightly over 200 men and suffered losses of 44%.[9]

During the slow pursuit of the defeated Confederates, the 145th once again entered Virginia. In late summer 1863, the regiment received its first influx of drafted soldiers. With their arrival the unit underwent a transformation; desertion became commonplace, and disciplinary problems began to increase. The unit was engaged in the Bristoe Station Campaign of October 1863, the Mine Run Campaign of November-December 1863, and then established winter camp near Germannia Ford.

During this second winter's camp, recruiting detachments returned to northwestern Pennsylvania in hopes of drawing new men into the depleted ranks. The regiment numbered over 700 as the spring campaign began. During fighting near the Spotsylvania Court House on May 12, 1864, the unit again suffered large losses: 22 men killed, 107 wounded, and an additional 37 missing.

On June 16, 1864, at Petersburg, Virginia, Lieutenant Colonel McCreary and 111 other officers and men of the regiment were captured. The rest of the regiment spent the long summer of 1864 in the trench warfare around Petersburg. All of the field officers were captured or killed by autumn 1864, and command of the regiment was in the hands of company grade officers. By January 1865 a mere 156 officers and men remained in the ranks of the 145th.

At the conclusion of the war, the regiment took part in the grand review in Washington D. C., and was mustered out of federal service on May 31, 1865. On June 5 the remnant of the regiment was welcomed home to Erie. After speeches by local politicians the regiment held its last parade and was dismissed for the final time.

No regimental history was ever compiled for this regiment. None of its members obtained national prominence or exceptionally high state office after the war, and there were never any best selling memoirs compiled by any of the survivors. The 145th Pennsylvania Volunteers simply fell into relative obscurity.

Stuckenberg and the 145th

Throughout his chaplaincy, Stuckenberg labored to provide for the spiritual as well as the physical needs of his soldiers. From the pages of his diary, it is clear that the position of chaplain was one that demanded a great deal of flexibility and one that was filled with numerous challenges. While organizing a regimental church to promote the Christian ideal in an environment not known for advancing Christian morality,

Stuckenberg also took time to secure and distribute packages from various aid societies to soldiers in the unit. The time he spent in correspondence with those societies secured, for the sick and wounded, medicines and foodstuffs that aided in their recovery or at least made the time spent in the hospital more comfortable.

Stuckenberg took an active role in the life of the regiment. He cared for the sick, dressing the wounds of those injured in combat, visiting and praying in the hospital tents, and most importantly projecting a strong moral presence in the camp. As a result of his "ministry of presence," a term in vogue among modern military chaplains, Stuckenberg's prestige among the officers and men grew. Throughout the pages of his diary, as well as in his unfinished regimental history, Stuckenberg's love for the soldier shines through. Not only would he conduct religious services for his own men, but he provided religious coverage to other regiments that needed pastoral care. Yet his concern for the men extended beyond mere religion. He took care of their physical and psychological needs, visiting those left behind in the various hospitals where they remained when the regiment moved. He provided a physical link between these men and their unit by assuring them that they were not forgotten.

Still it would be erroneous to suppose that Stuckenberg was not ultimately concerned with the state of his soldiers' souls. His evangelistic calling is amply demonstrated within these pages. Stuckenberg made sure that those who were sick or wounded had the opportunity to come to a personal relationship with their God. Many examples of conversion can be found within these pages, however, there are also glaring examples of his religious intolerance, particularly toward Catholics. Stuckenberg imparts an air of smug superiority over other chaplains with less formal and less intensive education. Thus, he concluded that Methodist Chaplains were "very clever, but lack cultivation."

The most revealing and perhaps most humanizing aspect of his diary are the numerous references concerning women. Although a man of the cloth, Stuckenberg—like any other young man of 28—had an eye for the ladies. What is unusual for the 19th century is that in addition to being attracted by physical beauty, Stuckenberg viewed women as nearly equal to men in intellect and spiritual beliefs.

Like many men of his era, Stuckenberg enlisted in the army with a romantic concept of war. After viewing the carnage of Antietam and after experiencing the regiment's decimation at Fredericksburg and Gettysburg, his views understandably changed. The anguish that he recorded over the death of men he persuaded into enlisting caused him to question the worthiness of the conflict, but never the necessity for it.

There may be times when the reader is surprised at the number of leaves of absence that the Chaplain was permitted to take. In every case they were not for personal enjoyment, but connected somehow with the administration of his churches or on behalf of the men of his regiment. Whether he was returning to Erie where he would conduct funeral services, or carrying tens of thousands of dollars of the men's pay to the banks in Washington, or visiting a fellow pastor along the line of march, Stuckenberg's ultimate concern was for the men of his regiment. The concern that he demonstrated for the soldiers endeared himself to them: he lived with them, shared the dangers of the battlefield with them, suffered through winter camp with them, and endured the hardship of the march with them. When his horse was killed after the battle of Chancellorsville, in May 1863, the officers and men of the regiment pooled their resources in order to raise the cash for him to purchase a new mount. Such a visible affirmation of the worth of his services deeply moved Stuckenberg and cemented his love towards the members of the 145th.

Officers are usually the butt of jokes and pranks by the enlisted men, and Stuckenberg was not exempt by virtue of his clerical rank. An amusing incident, related by Stuckenberg himself in his unfinished regimental history, shows that he could appreciate soldiers' humor and his own naivete. In the early days of the regiment's field duty, Stuckenberg, like so many other novice officers and men, brought along an excess of personal possessions that extended service in the field would prove to be utterly useless. Among the chaplain's possessions was an umbrella that provided a source of much amusement to the men and devilment to Stuckenberg. Having tried to rid himself of this useless item on numerous occasions, the ever-mindful soldiers of his regiment would locate and return it to him, accompanied, no doubt, by much mirth.[10]

During his military Service, Stuckenberg never ceased being pastor to his churches. Before his departure he took pains to assure his congregations that he would return as soon as his service to the army was no longer needed. Furthermore, the young cleric prepared sermons of sound theological content to be read during his absence. When the regiment departed on September 11, 1862, Stuckenberg was unable to accompany it because he had to make sure that everything was in order in his parishes before he departed. A vast amount of correspondence flowed between Stuckenberg and members of his congregations throughout the year; all dealt with church matters, and all pleaded for his permanent return. It was this deep concern for the congregations at home, combined with an increasing frustration with the incoming recruits in the fall of 1863, as well as his own questions concerning his effectiveness as a chaplain with these new conscripts, which led Stuckenberg to resign in October 1863.

As one reads the diary, the hardships of not only the regiment, but of this cleric become evident. His health was affected by camp life, long marches, poor food, and lack of rest. At the same time his keen sense of observation and of interpersonal relationships was developed. Although his official ties with the regiment were severed in October 1863, Stuckenberg continued to express concern for the religious health of his old comrades by donating money to the American Tract Society for religious material to be sent specifically to his former unit.[11]

With Stuckenberg's resignation, the 145th Pennsylvania Infantry lost its chief scribe and historian. Those who study this regiment keenly feel his loss. Erie's local papers were kept abreast of the regimental whereabouts and, in many instances, informed of the loss of a loved one by his frequent letters to the editors. His writings were for the most part extremely accurate and reflected his concern about his men. The name of every wounded man was spelled out and his condition described by one who had seen him.

There is no doubt in our minds that Stuckenberg's later scholarly work was influenced by his year as an army chaplain. It is, however, for other scholars to make the connection between his military experience and his social consciousness.

Editorial Policy

In editing this diary for publication we have attempted to faithfully reproduce Chaplain Stuckenberg's writing. Stuckenberg was a thoughtful writer, and there are very few instances where a word or phrase has been lined through and another substituted. We have chosen not to include the infrequent lined-out words. The diary is a combination of entries written almost immediately after the events described and entries written upon reflection days or weeks after the events described. For example the entry for October 27, 1862, and most of the entries from August 1863 were written almost immediately after the event. On the other hand, the description of the Fredericksburg attack of December 1862 was reconstructed several weeks into the new year.

Logical breakpoints in the text led to the creation of nine chapters. In a very few cases it has been necessary to rearrange the sequence of Stuckenberg's narrative so as to maintain a fairly strict chronological order. In some instances writings that are not part of the diary per se have been incorporated into the narrative. Those changes and additions are noted.

Stuckenberg's formation of new paragraphs is quite inconsistent: he would sometimes very slightly indent a paragraph; at times he would start a new line, although there was sufficient room on the preceding line to continue; at other times he would complete a multi-page entry with no obvious paragraphs. In the editing process we have divided the narrative into paragraphs as needed and have initiated paragraphs after all dated entries.

Some words abbreviated by Stuckenberg have been filled out and the inserted portions have been enclosed in square brackets [ ]. Some common abbreviations (e.g. Dr., lbs.) have been retained, and the abbreviations "ult." and "inst." (meaning "last" and widely used in nineteenth century writing) remain unchanged.

The ampersand (&) and the plus (+) symbols were used interchangeably in place of the word "and." All instances of this usage have been changed to "and."

Spelling inconsistencies (very few) are maintained, and in cases where confusion could result, "sic" is used to indicate Stuckenberg's spelling. Geographical names are spelled as rendered; if the spelling of a geographical name is not close to contemporary usage, it is footnoted.

Stuckenberg's punctuation—or lack thereof—has been retained. Underlining was infrequently used to indicate emphasis. It has been retained and appears in italics.

ACKNOWLEDGEMENTS

A great number of people have contributed to the publication of this diary. Had it not been for the detective work of theologian Richard Hoehn who rediscovered the diary, and the dedication of Barbara Hajek who sorted through many boxes of family papers, the Stuckenberg diary may well have been lost. Dr. Verel Salmon and Mr. Irwin Rider of the Erie Civil War Round Table opened their personal collections for our research as well as reviewing the draft of the transcription. Lucy Wolfe spent many hours at the word processor. John Stoudt and Brian Harvey—at the time, Gettysburg College students—also spent many hours at the word processor as well as assisting in verifying the transcription. Colleagues at Gettysburg College and in several other libraries and archives provided clues to identification of many of the individuals named in the diary. Special thanks go to: Mike Musick of the National Archives and Records Service; members of Luther Memorial Church, Erie; the staffs of the Erie County Historical Society, and the Erie Museum and Planetarium; J. R. Richards, Librarian Emeritus, Gettysburg College, and James Roach, Gettysburg National Military Park.

David T. Hedrick
Gettysburg, PA
Gordon Barry Davis Jr.
Erie, PA

CHAPTER

1

INTRODUCTION TO ARMY LIFE

"Oh God! How coust thou permit thy own creature to butcher each other so cruelly!"

September 11 - October 27, 1862

Bolivar Heights By Harper's Ferry Va Oct 6th 1862

On the 21st of July 1861 I went to Erie with the view of taking charge there. I organized an Engl[ish] Luth[eran] church in Erie on the 15th of August, and besides this, have two other churches in the charge—both German, the one 8 and the other 12 miles from Erie. Our success thus far has been far beyond our expectations.[1]

After an absence of three weeks, I returned to Erie on the evening of the 9th of September 1862. On the next day I applied for the chaplaincy of the 145 reg Pennsylvania vol and was appointed on the 11th inst.[2] The reg left Erie on the day of my appointment—I started the following Monday. I preached in all the churches of the charge on Sabbath the 14th inst. It was hard to part from my people and numerous friends, but they became somewhat reconciled to my going, when I promised to return to Erie, in case my life is spared. I have gained the deep and lasting affection of my people and am myself deeply attached to them.

I started with Capt Walker and company from Erie, to join the regiment.[3] At Harrisburg on the morning of the 17th a private in Walker's company (Dumars)[4] attempted to commit Suicide by stabbing himself 3 or 4 times and cutting his throat. We left him in a hospital in Harrisburg. We spent about a day in Chambersburg—after passing through the beautiful Cumberland valley—the Alleghenies on one and the Cumberland mountains on the other side. We found the people of Chambersburg very hospitable. On the 18th we arrived at Hagerstown. On the 19th I visited the battlefield of Antietam—by Sharpsburg—where one of the greatest—(if not the greatest) battle of this war was fought on the 17th inst.

The battle field extends about 4 or 5 miles in one direction and from 1- 2 in another. It is not level, but consists of a number of small hills with high depressions between them. On it were ploughed fields, stubble fields—corn fields and woods, and towards the Potomac is the village of Sharpsburg. The losses in this battle are supposed to be from 8000 to 10,000 wounded and killed on our side and more on that of the rebels.[5] The first regiment I saw on the battle field was the 111th Pa—from Erie.[6] I walked over a great part of the field. It was the first time in my life that I saw a battle field within a few days after the battle was fought. In many places the ground was torn up by shells and cannon balls. The ground was covered with cartridges, muskets, cannon and rifle balls, shells exploded and unexploded; grape, swords, bayonets, muskets knapsacks et cet.

A number of houses in Sharpsburg and others on the battle field were badly riddled—especially the Lutheran church in Sharpsburg in charge of Rev Startzman,[7] and a church (or schoolhouse?) standing in the woods about a mile from Sharpsburg. But the worst sight was that of the dead still lying on the field in great numbers. Never shall I forget that sickening sight. However sublime a battle field may be—after the fight the scene is very frightful and disgusting. Along a fence about the length of 20 rails I counted 60 dead bodies—mostly rebels—who can always be told by their grey clothing. They were lying so close to each other that their hand could have touched almost along the whole line—in fact it seems that they fell just as they stood in line of battle. Nearly all were lying on their backs, their faces turned up towards the sun, they looked bloated and were greatly swollen and most of them were black as the darkest negroes. From some wounds blood and putrid matter were still oozing. Wounds were seen on all parts of the body, a great many in the head and breast. From the body of one rebel, lying near Sharpsburg, the left leg was completely severed just about the thigh—a most horrid sight. The bodies looked the more frightful because they had been exposed to the hot sun for some 2 days when I saw them.

On the road near Sharpsburg I saw a rebel, wounded in the back part of the head, still breathing. Having been exposed to the hot sun for two days his face was bloated and his eyes closed with putrid matter. His mouth was open and his lips were parched. I poured a little water in his mouth which seemed to roll down his throat involuntarily, with a rattling gurgling noise. He breathed very slightly and moved his hands very little. This was the most affecting thing I saw. The next day I found that he had been removed. Sometimes the wounded lie 5 or 6 days on the field, without a drop of water and without having their wounds dressed. I turned from the sights, saying that compared with this to be killed outright is a mercy.

Many shells were found in yards and on the streets in Sharpsburg and I saw some boys amusing themselves by rolling cannon balls down a hill on the edge of the village. I had often imagined a battle field but never thought especially of the scene after the battle and could not have imagined it worse than it really is. I could not help exclaiming "Oh God! how coust thou permit thy own creature to butcher each other so cruelly!"

In Sharpsburg I saw Genl McClellan and many of the generals the same afternoon (the 19th). He looks young, but seems to be much worn and fatigued. He conversed quite pleasantly with a number of citizens who approached him, no doubt to give some information in reference to the enemy. We, (Capt Loomis and son and myself)[8] were hunting our regiment and enquired about its whereabouts at headquarters, but could learn nothing of it. We saw vast bodies of infantry, cavalry and artillery pass through Sharpsburg, all looking as if they were much in need of rest. We returned to Hagerstown about dark and slept, as the night before, in one of the passages of the Washington Hotel. We rode to Hagerstown with Capt Walker, who had been so fortunate as to find our regiment. We started for the battle field again early on Saturday morning and found our regiment near Sharpsburg, detailed to bury the dead. I was very glad to meet the regiment, and many, especially my own members were glad to see me. We remained on the battle field over Sunday, still burying the dead.

I expected to hold services Sunday morning but the regiment being away from camp I could not, so I distributed some tracts to those remaining and waited for their return. It did not seem like Sunday and many thought it was Saturday. Just before dark I wanted to hold services, but then we received marching orders and moved to the other side of

A Union burial detail at Antietam.

Sharpsburg. I was unwilling to close the day without some religious services, so we gathered around a large fire, sang some hymns, I offered a prayer, and made some remarks on 1st verse 23rd Ps[alms]. It was indeed a delightful meeting and all enjoyed it very much. Many eyes were moistened, all felt that we were still in God's hands. That night was the first I slept on the ground. I slept with Leut Col McCreary.[9] We kept on our clothes, and spread our blankets on some straw, opened an umbrella to protect us against the heavy dew. I got up the next morning with a cold, a sore back and knee. But this was only the beginning of sorrows. That afternoon we started for Harper's Ferry, traveled a very bad road, leading us up and down numerous hills, and part of the way along the banks of the Potomac. This afternoon I saw this historic stream for the first time. At night I lodged with a Mr. Nickles very near John Brown's former residence. We waded the Potomac and arrived at Harper's Ferry about noon on Tuesday.

Our regiment (145th Pa Vol) was placed in the Irish brigade Genl Meagher's, Hancock's division and Sumner's corps. The very fact of being placed in an Irish brigade was very displeasing to us, there being very few Irishmen in our regiment.[10]

Here the Irishmen in this brigade are rough, a week ago yesterday many were drunk, they were fighting et cet, and that after attending mass in the morning. Col Brown[11] said he had never seen such conduct permitted in the army before with impunity. Then the General—Meagher[12] (pronounced Marr) is very profane and I am told frequently gets beastly drunk. At one of the battles they say (At Antietam I believe) he was so drunk that he fell from his horse.[13] One of his staff whilst drunk was insulting, abusing, and threatening our men of a few days ago. Poor fellow, he caries his arm in a sling now and looks very wretched, he fell from his horse I believe, while drunk. Yesterday he was in a wagon and wanting to get out one of our men very kindly ran to assist him, he rejected his offer with the words "Go to hell!" He looks as if he were there already. One evening last week, about eleven o'clock they seemed to have a regular row in one of the tents near the General's. Oath succeeded oath, threat followed threat. They were very loud and boisterous and apparently very much excited, and I am very much mistaken if they did not pound each other. It lasted for about an hour, and kept me as well as the Lieut Col awake a long time.

A rather amusing scene occurred that week. One morning three of our men were going after water or down to the river to wash, when somebody, attending to a call of nature cried out: halt. Two stopped, the other went on. Up jumped the man, buttoned his pants, caught hold of the fellow that did not halt, who on the other hand caught hold of the man's throat and handled it not very gently. It happened to be his great excellency, the general, who called his Major, had the fellow arrested, and tied to a tree, "to teach him" as the general said, 'who I am.' The soldier it seems, did not know him as the general did not have his uniform on.

One morning I heard some angry words near the Genl's tent—some one saying: 'If he says another word, take my pistol and shoot him!' The guard was then called and told: 'If he will not go, run a bayonet through him!' What the poor fellow had done, I know not. Perhaps he was the fellow who had stolen some goods from a sutler, and who

Introduction to Army Life

Colonel Hiram L. Brown in the uniform of a Brevet Brigadier General.

was soon after tied hands and feet—and then tied to a tree, and had, they say a rusty bayonet thrust through his mouth to gag him.

A week ago yesterday the Genl issued an order to all the regiments to this effect: "The Catholics will, and all others may attend mass in a church in Harper's Ferry, that morning." This was issued without consulting any of us. This order was very offensive to the chaplain of the Mass regiment.[14] (which was placed temporarily in this brigade, but has been in it some 4 months) and also to myself, because we thought the genl had no business to issue such an order without consulting us. But from the 145th not a single man went not even the Catholics; but all attended our service in the afternoon—when I preached on the "profanity" which prevailed to a dreadful extent, but has sensibly diminished since then.[15]

When in Chambersburg with Capt Walker's Co[mpany] I was requested to address them. After singing a hymn and making a short address, just as I said "Let us pray" an Irishman, very innocently, and no doubt sincerely said "Three cheers for the Parson". All was solemn during the rest of the services, but the poor fellow, frequently heard about it afterwards. The cheers were, of course, not given. Last Saturday about noon, this same man came to me with a testament in his hand, which he had borrowed from a tent mate. He had been attending our evening meetings, which had been very serious—especially the one held in the company to which he belonged on the evening previous. He told me he had been a Catholic all of his life. That a few days ago, he had seen one of the Catholic chaplains (of whom there are three in the brigade) who had asked him, why he did not attend mass on last Sabbath? He replied: I wanted to attend the service of our own chaplain. The priest replied that he had no business to do so. But the priest seems to have had little influence over him. I saw that he felt deeply. He confessed he was a sinner and could find forgiveness not through the Priest—but only through Christ. He had never read a testament before, and with tears in his eyes told me how he loved the book—though he had only read it since morning. He told me: 'I am a Catholic now no more. I belong to your church.' After talking to him on the subject a little more, giving him advice and exhorting him to read the Bible, he left fully determined from this time to be an Evangelical Christian, and to pay no attention to what the Priest might say.

Bolivar Heights near Harper's Ferry Oct 12th 1862

This is the first Sabbath that we have had no religious services in which the whole regiment could join. I wanted service at 11 A.M. but the Lt Col thought it better to postpone it till immediately after dress parade as there would be more of the regiment present then. I assented but just as they were about having dress parade it commenced raining, and it still rains. So we could hold no services which is a great disappointment to me. But I taught a Bible class in Capt Wood's Camp,[16] visited the hospital in town this afternoon and held services in three rooms, which were certainly beneficial—and I also held services in the hospital in camp. This does not seem much like Sabbath, but it surely is not my fault.

Heavy firing has been heard today—supposed to be at Point of Rocks—some twelve miles east of this place. What the result is I have not yet learned. The rebels are again in P[ennsylvani]a and have possession of Mercersburg and Chambersburg. But McClellan's cavalry have gone in pursuit of them.[17]

Yesterday was the first day that was really fall-like. The wind was chilly, there was a mist hanging over the mountains all day, and generally it seemed as if "The melancholy days had come, the saddest part of the year."[18] Thus far it has been very hot and sultry during the day, but generally cold at nights. Indeed, I think we had but few days last summer in Erie which were hotter than the weather has been here ever since we came, till yesterday. A week ago yesterday Lieut Wittich,[19] received a sunstroke—and yet at midnight it was so cold that I could scarcely keep warm. The dews are very heavy, so that neither tents nor india rubber blankets are a perfect protection against them. There has been and still is a great deal of sickness in camp, sometimes as many as 150 taking medicine. This is owing to various causes. The season itself is not the most healthy. Then the difference [between] the temperature of day and night is so very great. The water is not very good, though I am told it is much worse farther down in Virginia. Then the food is not the best—hard, old crackers—with living creatures and pork alive with skippers.[20] Then sleeping on the ground and change of life generally are calculated to provoke sickness. I have been unwell myself for about two weeks—with a bad cold; but am better now. The prevailing diseases are: diarrhea, dysentery, rheumatism, measles and colds.

There are two men in Co A who tried to get me to use my influence to get discharged from the service. Both of them have been married for some years; and yet such are the pernicious effects of the early indulgences, that now they frequently have nocturnal emissions, foul dreams etc.—besides rheumatism and general debility—such as renders them unfit for service. There are evidently many here who ought never to have been permitted to enlist as they are utterly unfit for service. Some seem to have been conscious of the fact and enlisted merely for the sake of the bounty. Surely there are many motives besides Patriotism to lead men in the army. And many who are here would gladly return home, never again to enlist in the service of their country.

According to a late order no commissioned officer is to leave the camp without permission from the Genl. Capt Wood went to Genl Meagher this morning to get permission to visit a friend near Harper's Ferry. The Genl received him very rudely by saying: "I want you to learn that you can approach me only through my adjutant." He went to the adjutant, but of course received no permission to go. Soon after this I approached the Genl through the Major, for the purpose of getting permission to leave camp at any time, so that I might visit the hospital. After some little unwillingness manifested by the Genl he gave me permission—so I go where and when I please.

Bolivar Heights by Harper's Ferry Va Oct 16th 1862

Early this morning the Irish Brigade, our regiment excepted, and a number of other brigades went out on a reconnoitering expedition. After they were gone about an hour heavy firing was heard some 4 miles away from here. I stood at Bolivar Heights and could see the smoke rising from the guns fired as well as the smoke produced by the burning of shells. I was very desirous of being on the ground, but thought I had no business there and did not go. I know that some rebel officers were captured, and that our boys advanced; but have heard of nothing further.[21]

There was plenty of excitement, noise, quarreling and swearing in some of the Irish regiment last night, which kept me awake for some time. At nine some newsmessenger was running with all of his might, a whole host of Irishmen after him throwing stones, bottles et cet., and threatening to kill him. He was afterwards rescued from them, but I did not learn what was done with him. Whether they had stolen from him (which seems most likely) or whether he had stolen from them I did not learn. One however, would exasperate them about as much as the other.

Some of our men are very sick, Henry Fidler[22] being the worst of all. I saw him about noon. He stared at me and moved his lips but could not speak. His case is considered very doubtful, his disease being typhoid—or, as it is called here, camp fever. Lieuts Wittich, Espy,[23] and Parker[24] are also very sick. I saw the last named this afternoon. He asked me to pray with him, which I cheerfully complied with. He then told me of his grandmother (or mother?) who was dependant on him, and he seemed to worry much about her. By his side lay the son of Capt Loomis also very sick. The accommodations are very poor for the sick in camp. They sleep on the ground with perhaps a few spruce twigs and a blanket under them, exposed to the heat in the day and to cold at nights. It is enough to make a well man sick and well calculated to keep a sick man from getting well. Then they are not waited on as they should be, though I find their comrades very kind to them. Neither can they get all the things they sometimes have an appetite for. And the Doctors have been so unfortunate as not to receive any medicines from the government yet, so that for many they could do very little or nothing at all. With all these things comes the intense longing to be home, which is never so deep and intense as when sick. Then we appreciate the kindness of relatives and friends as we never did before. As we have nothing else to occupy our minds they are continually thinking of them. Our imagination paints the scenes of home to our mental eye; we remember the joys there experienced and every kind look and word and attention and contrast them with our present condition. Then sickness is calculated to make the heart tender and deepens love. And I often hear the expression: "If only I could be at home." "If my mother, my wife, my sister were only here." And however kind others may be they can never take the place of these. There are no doubt many whose only chief ailing is homesickness.

I see the sick quite frequently and am always welcome. I try to minister both to their spiritual and secular wants as well as I can. They are most easily influenced during illness and I try to point them to Christ if not yet his. But I am persuaded that during health is the time to seek the Lord. Fear of death is so apt to be the strongest motive to become a professor during sickness; and the impressions made there are so apt to be but transitory.

Though I have a good many calls I am in my tent most of the time, and have often been asked whether I don't get lonely. I am so accustomed to being alone that there is but little danger of this. I read some daily paper, write a good many letters, and read Macauley's Essays or Fichte's Lectures to the German Nations[25] or busy myself with everything else that is interesting. Indeed the danger is not that I will not have visitors enough, but too many. There is however, something lonely and dreary about a tent especially on an evening like the present. Most of the men are away either with the reconnoitering party or out on picket, so there is but little noise, except that produced by falling rain on my tent, which makes the evening gloomy. My only companions are numerous flies and long legged spiders now and then running over me or along the side of my tent; and by my side is a grasshopper, who has been quietly sitting there for some time sheltered from the rain. He is my nearest neighbor just now and as I have gained a kind of affection for him on this account I do not disturb him.

My furniture is very simple, a bedstand of my own construction, which also answers as a seat during the day, though back is wanting. On it lie some oak leaves, a few newspapers, an overcoat and pair of pants, on which I sleep. My every day coat is my pillow, my woolen and india rubber blankets and my shawl form my cover. At night I wear woolen socks (and still my feet are very cold every night), drawers, undershirt, nightcap and gown. To my left stands my large trunk, well packed with necessaries, most of which, however, I shall most likely have to leave behind me as we are allowed only 25 lbs. baggage. A barrel standing on end is my writing desk and an empty cracker box is my only portable seat. My carpet consists of pine twigs, now mostly trampled to pieces. If I am contented, my tent is large enough, my furniture sufficient for me to be perfectly happy. If I am not contented a palace magnificently furnished would leave me miserable.

We have had two flags presented to our regiment, one by the ladies of Erie and the other by the State of Pennsylvania. Both are very beautiful. The former was presented by Lt Col and [received] by Col; the latter was presented by Col Thomas[26] and [received] by Col but Lt Col made the speech, Col Brown being a man of action and no speech maker.

An excellent letter from Dr. Stohlman[27] of N.Y. this evening. I wrote to Miss Elizabeth Ketchaus[28] the 6th inst. Will she reply? I only met her a few times when in Indianapolis lately, but I liked her very much, and I hope she will not object to a correspondence.

Bolivar Heights Va Oct 17th 1862

"Strike tents" was the order given to the Irish Brigade (our regiment excepted) and was immediately obeyed. They were ordered to Charles Town, which it was expected, would be held by our troops. This afternoon, however, all the baggage wagons returned and the report came that our troops were leaving Charles Town again. Tonight, I am told, the troops in camp are all ordered to sleep on their arms but this may be a mistake. The Charles Town affair is, I suppose, what is termed a "skedaddle."

I attended a soldier's funeral this afternoon. He was from NJ. A Connecticut Chaplain read some passages of Scripture, made a few remarks and offered a prayer.

A squad of his own company were there, a few officers and a number of spectators. A brother, also a soldier, was the only relative and real mourner. He wept bitterly.

H. Fidler is no better. He became so restless, that his couch was removed and his bed made on the floor. His eyes are very clear and bright. The surroundings of the eye were not so livid as yesterday, and his look generally was better then yesterday, owning perhaps to a fever on him this afternoon. There is little hope of his recovery. In one of the rooms I was requested to make a prayer, which I was glad to do. I then left the hospital and visited most of those who are sick in their tents. Some were very sick and had very poor accommodations, lying almost on the bare ground, their heads on their knapsacks. Their food is not very good, consisting chiefly of hard crackers, rice, sometimes fresh meat; besides this, they sometimes purchase some bread and other things. Various diseases prevail—such as diarrhea and dysentery, measles, and typhoid fever. Many, I find, have hot fevers and are apt to be flighty.

I heard an explosion this afternoon, looked to the spot and saw a cloud of smoke. I just now learned that a fire had been built over a place where a shell lay buried, which becoming heated exploded. 4 men I am told were killed, and some wounded, but this I don't believe.

Bolivar Heights, Va Sunday Oct 19th 1862

As most of our men were out on picket and did not return till about 4 A.M. I could hold no services with the regiment during the day. I however held services in the wards of the hospitals and with Lts Wittich and Parker, and conducted the services in 29 Mass this morning. About dark I went to all the companies and informed them we were to have services; it was pleasant though not as many present as we usually have on Sabbath. I then conducted a Bible Class in Co I. So that altogether I held religious exercises ten different times today.

In one of the wards in the division hospital I found an aged German, who spoke no English. He was very glad to see me, as there seemed to be none to whom he could talk. He belongs to the Lutheran Church.

Lt Wittich, though not a member of any church, was very glad to have me hold services with him, and told me how he had been touched when his little girl 6 years old had asked her mother why her papa did not pray at table? When I spoke on the subject of religion he said, he did not know whether a man as sick as he was in a fit state of mind to reflect much on the subject.

Yesterday Mr. Danson spoke about being baptized; but as he thought he could live as well out of the church as in it, I advised him to wait. He then told me that his Father, a professed Lutheran had never prayed to his knowledge, though he had lived at home for 23 years. A sad fact—especially when related by an unconverted son. His Father attends our Fairview church.

Lt Col McCreary has just learned by telegraph that his father is dead and feels the stroke quite severely. And a private of Co K came to me this evening to see whether

I would not use my influence to get him a furlough to go home, as his wife was not expected to live. So we find that not only do persons die in the army, but also when at home, surrounded by friends and enjoying all the comforts and attention they could wish.

Bolivar Heights Oct 20th 1862

Today I performed the ceremony of baptism—the first time in camp, and the first time in my life by immersion. I tried to persuade Mr. Richardson[29] to be sprinkled; but I could not succeed. He prefers immersion, believes it to have been the Apostolical method, and thinks it the true mode of baptism, while he does not condemn sprinkling. As any mode if properly performed is to me baptism, and as the N.T.[30] prescribes no particular one, I thought it my duty to yield to his preferences. I have often discussed the mode of baptism and have said there might be cases when I would immerse; this was one of them. Then I am in camp, minister to the spiritual wants of men of all denominations, and cannot act as I would in a Lutheran or any denominational church. Whether my brethren in the ministry would justify or condemn my course I do not know. But that is a small matter, since I acted conscientiously on the subject and did my duty.

In letters from Erie my friends are imploring me to return. It seems that little will be done at church building while I am gone, at least for a while. But I am here and expect to remain in the army as long as I can. My trust is in God. Hence I do not fear in reference to myself as much as my friends. When three years ago I went to Germany I felt sure that God would be my Shepherd and would restore me safely to my friends in America. I have that same confidence in him now. And so much fear and anxiety are to me indications of lack of faith and confidence in God. He will preserve me and restore me to my people. If not—He knows best. "Was Gott thut das ist wohlgethan."[31]

Testaments have come from Erie for our Regiment, and all seem to be glad at receiving the Word of Life, even those who are positively wicked. May it prove to them a great blessing and be the means of saving many souls from destruction.

Bolivar Heights, Oct 22nd 1862

In visiting the sick this afternoon I was much affected at the sight of Mr. Gorman[32] suffering from camp fever. His countenance was fearfully distorted and indicated derangement of the mind. He seemed to be greatly tormented—tortured with pain. He twisted and turned his body, raised himself up and threw himself down again, clenched his fist, rolled his eyes, doubled his tongue red below, parched and cracked and bloody above and bit it apparently from pain. I could not but pity the poor fellow, and was sorry I could not relieve his sufferings. And as I left I could not help thinking, that such might be my condition some day. God in mercy prevent it! I have diarrhea and headache now and know not what may follow.

Members of his regimental Church 1862.

Harper's Ferry, Va. Oct 5th 1862
Camp of the 14th Regt. Pa. Vol.

We the undersigned members of various Christian Denominations, desiring to promote each others growth in Grace and Spiritual welfare generally, do hereby form ourselves into a regimental Church adopting the Bible as our only rule of Faith and Practice, and promising, in whatever circumstances we may be, to be faithful to our Christian Profession.

Names.	Denominations	Residence.
J. H. W. Stuckenberg	Lutheran	Erie, Pa. — Chaplain
John Trunsdell	M E Church (Ma)	Conneaut Erie Co PA
Marvin Gilson	M. E. Church	Steam Mills Warren Co Pa
David McKinley	M. E. Church (Ma)	Tidioute Warren Co Pa
Cyrus J. Richardson	M. P. Church (Ma)	Fillmore Fillmore Co. Min.
Charles W Grove	M E Church (Ma)	Tionesta Venango Pa
Lewis Bimber	Wesleyan Meth. (Ma)	Tidioute Warren County Pa
A C Williams	Wesleyan Meth (Ma)	Tidioute Warren Co pa
James M. Batchelor	E Methodist (Ma)	New Hamburgh Mercer Co
Dyer Loomis	Presb. N.S. (Ma)	North East — Capt.
David Webber	Lutheran (Ma)	Erie, Pa.
M. W. Oliver (Artillery)	Pres N.S.	Spring Crawford Co Pa Capt
James A McElroy	Baptist Co I. (Ma)	Blakelyville Mercer Co
Ino W Reynolds	Episcopal Church	Erie Captain
W W W Wood	O.S. Presbyterian Ma	West Greenville Captain
Simeon Bond	N.S. Presbyterian Co D.	Springfield X Roads Erie Co. Pa.
Calvin Hall	M. E. Church Co C	Mooreheadville Erie Co. Pa.
Andrew F. Ennis	Erie Baptist Church	Arcadia Wain Co N.Y.
J B Fickinger	Lutheran Co I	Erie Penna
J D Cochran	M E Church (Co C Ma)	Wattsburgh Erie Co Pa
Andrew J Long	United Pres Lytherian	Sheakleyville Mercer Co. Pa.
C H Johnson	Congregational Co D	Sterritania Erie Co Pa
Charles Cole	Church of England	London England Co. E Pa
W A Arms	Not United Co F	
V. A. Long	M. E. Church Co I West	Millcreek Erie Co. Pa.
J. A. McPherrin	M. E. Church Co I	West Greenville Mercer Co
R B Warnock	M E Church (Ma) Co I	West Greenville Mercer Co Pa
S. P. Smith	Evangelical Association Co G	Orangeville Trumbull Co Oh

Members of the Regimental Church, October 5, 1862.

Introduction to Army Life

Names	Denomination	Post Office	Company	
Elijah Foster	Freewill Baptist	Waterford, Erie Co.	C.	Ma.
Calvin Pier (missing)	M. E. Church	Corry Erie Co	Com. D	
Ch. Ed. Hoyt	M. E. Church	Union Mills Erie Co. Pa.	E.	
John S. Osborn (killed)	M. E. Church	Summit Erie Co. Pa.	Com. B	
Wm. U. Brown	Lutheran Erie Pa	Erie Pa	J	
D. B. McCreary	O. S. Pres. Church (Park Church)	Erie Pa	Lt. col.	Ma
T. C. Crook	M. E. Church	Erie Pa	D.	
Newton Hatfield	Baptist	Sheakleyville Pa	y	
John H. Clingan	United Presbyterian	Harthegig Mercer Co	g	Ma
Thomas E. Clingan	U. S. Presbyterian	Harthegig Mercer Co	G	
David Davis (killed)	Baptist	Westgeenville Mercer Co	G	Ma
Andrew E. Ilster	Methodist E.	Harthegig Mercer Co	G	
George W. Poole (killed)	Methodist E.	North Mills Mercer Co	G	
T. F. McCreary 1st Lieut	Methodist E.	Clarksville Mercer Co Pa	Co G	
G. R. McCreary	M. E.	Erie Pa	D	
S. F. Ware	M. E.	West Springfield Erie Co.	D	
James U. Southward	Baptist Freewill	North East Erie Co	G.	Ma
James H. Bogue	M. E. Church	Wattsburg Erie Co.	C.	Ma
Samuel D. Dean	M. E. Church	West Springfield Erie Co.	Co K	Ma
J. W. Hill	M. E. Church	Wayne Erie Co Pa.	A.	Ma
S. Hayberger	M. E. Church	Erie Pa	D	
C. B. Farver	Lutheran	Erie Pa	J	
D. L. King	M. E. Church	Union Mills Erie Co	E.	
Capt Chas M. Lynch	Episcopal	Erie City	D	
Lieut J. W. Vincent	United Presby.	West Greenville Pa	G.	Ma
D. W. Webster	United Presby	Sheakleyville Mercer Co Pa	G	Ma
J. C. Dalrymple	M. E. Church	Wattsburg Erie Co. Pa.	K.	Ma.
J. H. Richardson	Regimental Lutheran Church	Tidioute Warren Co Pa	Co F	Ma
Wilbur F. Kinsley	M. E. church	Espyville Crawford Co Pa	Co H	
J. H. Espy	do do	do do	do	
Geo. A. Stephenson	do do	Chagrin Falls Cuyahoga Co Ohio		Ma
George C. Evans		Erie Pa		

658 names

Bolivar Heights, Va Oct 27th 1862

On the morning of the 23rd I was told: 'Fidler is dying!' I hastened over to the hospital and found him lying very still, one hand on his face the other before him on the bed. His hands were blue and cold, his eyes fixed, though he looked very natural—excepting the brown matter flowing from his nose and mouth. He had great difficulty in breathing. We knelt down in prayer and committed his soul to God. After we had [finished], he still breathed but only at great intervals—and soon he ceased breathing altogether.[33] There was no change of countenance, not a muscle was moved. His eyes remained the same, though the lids no longer closed. He died so gently that we did not even know he was dead, and still expected him to draw another breath, when we found that his spirit had already taken its flight. Capt Brown[34] and Lt Griswold[35] were also there. With tearful eyes we watched him as he passed through the dark valley of the shadow of death. This was the first time in my life I saw a grown person die and could not help exclaiming "Such is death!" How can death be called the King of Terrors when he comes in so mild a manner? Surely, He can be such to the wicked only. I almost envied Henry Fidler his gentle departure into the other world.

On the 24th 5 P.M. his body was buried in the graveyard on Bolivar Heights. His coffin was of rough boards, carried by six members of his company. It was preceded by a fifer playing a funeral tune, by the Lt Col, myself and 4 soldiers carrying their muskets reversed, and was followed by the officers and men of the company to which he had belonged and by others. I read some passages of Scripture at the grave, made some remarks and offered a prayer. The coffin was let down in the grave, a volley of four muskets fired over his grave, the benediction pronounced and the grave filled—the head and foot thereof being marked with boards. I then made a long letter to his father giving a full account of his sickness, death and burial, also indicating the spot on which the body was buried.

Whilst our regiment was being formed in Erie I was frequently requested to make war speeches, for the purpose of furthering enlistments. I did so twice. The first time Wm Brown,[36] George Evans[37] and Daniel Farver[38] and two others enlisted. The second time Henry Fidler enlisted. I often debated the question: whether it was right for me to try to persuade men to go—as those thus persuaded might be the very ones that would never return. Henry Fidler is the first one that died in the regiment from sickness (some one, I believe, has died in the regiment from the accidental discharge of a musket, not here but in Chambersburg). But from what I can learn, he would have gone anyhow, whether I had made that speech or not. He wanted to go some months ago, but his father objected. I never tried to persuade any particular individual to enlist—but appealed to all in general.

Well do I remember with what affection his sister regarded Henry, as she was standing in the photograph gallery with him, the day he left Erie. It was a sad, a long and last farewell.

On the night of the 24th Gorman died. I was told by the doctor that his apparent sufferings were not real as he was unconscious. May not his sufferings have made him unconscious? I was also told by the doctor that evil practices had had much to do with the progress of his disease. What a horrid, soul and body destroying sin! The body was buried yesterday with short religious service at the grave.

Yesterday it rained all day—was chilly and fall like. No regimental services could be held. In the afternoon I, however, held services in the hospital. I also visited the room in which Last Sabbath found a German who spoke no English. I at once looked for him, but found his bed empty. On inquiry I found he had died during the week and also another sick soldier who was there last Sunday. Having no chaplain they had had no services at their graves. I requested to nurses to let me know of such occasions and I would gladly conduct the services. A number of our men are still very sick others are recovering very slowly. The doctor told me this morning there are "only" 117 on the sick list—and thinks the health of the regiment is decidedly improving.

Physicians are very apt to be very much hardened and not only to manifest little or no sympathy for their patients, but to treat them harshly and rudely. Dr. P[39] told me the other day that he had enough to do with killing patients—he could not attend to them afterwards. I fear there is too much ground for the complaints of our men, that they are much neglected, often cursed and very inhumanly treated. I cannot visit the sick and well as often as they want me to do. This has generally been the case with me wherever I have been—from this quarter the first and perhaps only complaint came. Yet I am about a good deal, especially with the sick. And I think they cannot reasonably complain. Some seem to think I must be about all the time.

The Ladies Sold[ier's] Aid Soc[iety] of Erie and the Col have placed the hospital stores in my charge. Some seem to think the sick do not at present get as much of them as they are entitled too. This is throwing new responsibilities on me—but I trust I can meet them faithfully.

I have made a rude kind of heating apparatus which does remarkably well, if the wind comes from the North. Otherwise there is more smoke than fire in my tent. I had a pleasant time of it last night. The wind blowing hard loosened the tent pins in the soft ground and threatened to blow my tent away. At about 2 A.M. I went out in the rain, cold and wind and drove the pins down with a brick—and tied some ropes to a heavy box back of the tent. All right this morning—but wind high and tent again threatened. All around are driving in their pins. I must take some dinner.

Bol[ivar] H[eights] Oct 27th 1862. 9 1/2 PM.

About an hour ago a soldier came to my tent saying: 'Capt Loomis would like to have you go to the hospital with him, one of our men is dying.' I immediately went and found Milton Ward[40] struggling with death. There were 5 or 6 other patients in the room, Capt L[oomis], two men of Company C besides the nurses. M[ilton] W[ard] was lying very quietly, his eyes closed, mouth open. He breathed with great difficulty—and with a loud rattling (death rattle) in his throat. I proposed prayer, but it was feared it might wake Lt Parker, lying next to Ward—so I requested silent prayer. There we stood around that dying bed, each imploring God to have mercy on the soul of the dying youth. He drew his last breath, a feeble one, about 9 o'clock. It was an easy death, he being asleep, though not as easy as that of Fidler. A friend of his took it very hard, and seemed to be especially anxious about his soul—Ward having been rather wild and careless. Seeing him die made me reflect on my own death. The fact that I must die became to me living and real. I thought of myself lying thus surrounded by friends, perhaps by strangers, perhaps all alone, looking for the last time on the objects of time, bidding them a last farewell, and going home. I could see myself breathing with great difficulty, and imagine what thoughts would come in such an hour. I fear not death—still it has terrors for the stoutest heart. The worst is—leaving so many dear friends to mourn your loss. But they too must all follow before long. I thought after leaving the death scene of what I ought to be—pure, holy, ever angelic. No evil, too trifling, no carelessness should be indulged. What a spur to duty is such a scene! Souls to be saved—it is too late when leaving the clay, perhaps too late during sickness. What a value has time! It is short—therefore I should use every moment. It will soon be gone never to be recalled. Lessons of wisdom may be learned at the dying bed. Lord! "So teach us to number our days, that we may apply our hearts unto wisdom." 'Father in heaven—Grant that my end may be peaceful and hopeful, that death may lose its sting and the grave its victory.'

CHAPTER

2

MOVING SOUTH TO FREDERICKSBURG

"I know that my heart was not made for this."

October 28 - December 9, 1862

Warrenton Va Nov 10, 1862

 A grand Review took place near Bolivar Heights on the 29th ult. On the evening of the same day we received marching orders. All was hurry and confusion till we left. As the moon was shining brightly it was pleasant marching. We went about 4 miles and encamped on the east of Loudon Heights. As it was cold, Capt Walker and I went into a corn field and as an order was issued that the corn must not be taken away each of us crept into a shock. It was no doubt better than the bare ground, but by no means the most comfortable bed I ever slept in. Next day we marched to Braddock's Road, where we pitched out tents.

 I took several meals at the house of a rather well to do farmer the first secesh in whose house I ate. He had a good looking wife who was very active. He also had several slaves an old man, a young, good looking mulatto woman, the wife of the old darkey. The woman had a number of children, almost white, one fine looking little boy was indeed quite white around the mouth and nose. I can never believe they were the old mans' children. The white man's name was Conrad.

 I went back to Harper's Ferry from this place on wagon train at 11 1/2 P.M. Oct 31st for the purpose of visiting our sick, of whom we had left a great many at the Ferry, and of distributing to them some of the Hospital stores sent in my care by the Ladies of Erie. Two of my members were left there, J. Fickinger,[1] and Wm Brown both of them very dear to me. Some person had stolen a box of the "Stores", but I found it again though more than half emptied.

 I visited all our sick in the hospitals and found that those in the Lutheran Church hospital had been shamefully neglected, as with three or four exceptions no physician had been near any of them. They were glad to see me and were anxious to have me stay, which I could not, however, do. Mrs. Lt Wittich went with me and assisted me in distributing the stores. It brought tears to my eyes to see so many suffering so, and having so little attention paid them and so few of the comforts of life.

As I had not slept any the night before and had run about all day, ministering to the sick, I felt very tired in the afternoon and was urged by Mrs. Wittich, and by Mrs. and Miss Coleman (at whose house I took my breakfast while at the Ferry) to remain till morning. But I feared our regiment would move on and perhaps get into a battle, so I started from the ferry at 4.20 P.M. I got a chance to ride several miles in an ambulance. When I got to our camp I found that the regiment had gone so I started in pursuit and walked at a quick rate till nearly nine o'clock. As I was very tired and still some miles from our regiment I went into a house and staid there for the night. The old lady and son in law (Mr. Hagar) and one daughter were strong secesh. The other daughter was Union, her husband a Un[ited] Breth[ern] preacher, being in our army. Mrs. Hagar asked me whether I considered slavery a sin; on replying that I did, she became very much incensed and asked me whether I took the Bible for my guide?[2]

I ate a hearty supper and breakfast, slept well and started next morning, pretty early, and soon came up with our regiment. It was Sunday, but nothing indicated it. When near Snickersville the regiments were suddenly drawn up in battle lines. I cast my eyes over the beautiful valley before me, where all seemed to be so quiet and peaceful—a Sabbath seemed to rest upon the land. Skirmishers were sent out—we marched up a hill and by noon had possession of Snicker's Gap. Just as we got there, the rebels were seen hurrying thither from the other side of the mountain. Only about 200 rebel cavalry were in the Gap just before we took it—who skedaddled as we approached. Our battery shelled the rebels who did not reply. I saw a number of their cavalry moving to and fro, but do not know whether any were hurt.

We left the Gap in the even[ing] and encamped near Snickersville for the night. It was a cold, windy night, but I was pretty comfortable as I slept with Rev Wilson, chapl[ain] of 81 P[ennsylvania],[3] who had plenty of blankets. On 3rd inst. I rested at the house of a widow—Mrs. Carter, who was very much troubled about her chickens et cet. being taken by our soldiers. I there saw a Mrs. Tennyson, whose niece Miss Myers, married a brother of Dr. Mayill of Erie. Slept with Bro[ther] Wilson again, under a haystack. Lay still nearly all day Tuesday—only moving our quarters about 1/4 mile.

5th inst. I got tired in the evening and as my feet were sore, I went into a house by the side of the road and put up there for the night. Family—Mr. and Mrs. Furgueson and baby 7 months old (Adjutant[4] avers another baby coming soon.) Mrs. F[urgueson] decidedly the most beautiful woman I have seen for months—one of the most beautiful I ever saw. Small in size, quick in motion, beautiful in every expression,—indeed all who saw her admired her beauty. How he ever got her I cannot tell.

Crossed Manassas Gap railroad on 6th at Piedmont station, and camped near Rectortown two nights. Snow, ice, wind, very cold on the 7th. Left Rect[or]town on

8th. I was very sick that morning and could scarcely move about when I got up. I was, therefore, soon compelled to get into an ambulance. I was still quite sick yesterday and very weak, but I walked during the whole march of about four hours, carrying besides my canteen and haversack three blankets. But I came very near dropping down beside the road several times. We camped near Warrenton in which place I slept last night in a warm, soft bed. This is the first time I was in a bed since 21st Sept. I feel like stopping and eulogizing beds—but I will leave that for some other time. I am much better today—though I have very little appetite and am still weak.

McClellan having been removed from his command, (what position he is to occupy now I know not) he held a farewell review. It was in every respect a grand affair—and sublime spectacle. The cheering of the troops was most vociferous. Many officers declare they will resign if Mc[Clellan] is laid aside for political reasons or is laid aside at all. He is evidently much beloved, has the unbounded confidence of those who served under him, and is the hero and idol of our army.

Camp near Warrenton Va Nov 12th 1862

I learned today of the death of two more young men belonging to regiment—Lamertine,[5] son of Capt Loomis, who died a week ago last Monday, and Bemis,[6] a member of Co I. Both were quite young—about 17. Lamertine was a very fine boy, in whom very properly much affection and many hopes were centered. Kind and obliging and loving, he was a source of comfort and gratification to his father in the camp. His motives for enlisting were, no doubt, of the purest kind. It was soon found, however, that he was too tender to endure the hardships of soldier life. He became pale, his eyes looked sunken and languid, his step became less sprightly, his energy seemed to grow less and less, at last he sank down with camp fever. His father took him home, but his spirit could not be retained in his feeble frame. Though not a professor he was, I believe, a true Christian and died in peace and with hope. Most keenly does his father feel his loss. I said today to him, "He falls a sacrifice to his country, without engaging in a single battle," he replied—"Yes and without being of any service to his country." I learned to love Lamertine and feel sad at his loss—which is no doubt his gain.

Bemis was no professor of religion. But when I spoke to him a week ago last Saturday about his soul and asked him "whether he as ready to die and meet his God?" he answered firmly and cheerfully "Yes." His lips was parched, his eyes were sunken, his cheeks were hollow as he had fallen away a great deal.[7] I left him with the sad feeling that I should never see him again.

Our Col is an excellent man, but he is too fond of strong drink. Were he left to himself, he would, most likely let it alone. But the Adjutant, who exerts great influence over him and is a kind of pet, is greatly to blame as he is sometimes the means of procuring for him liquor. Yesterday these two as well as the Quartermaster[8] seem to have been indulging too much—a fact that has become well known among the officers and men and is exerting its evil influence.

Dr. Potter, Chief Surgeon of our Regiment, also drinks, and is accused of taking whiskey that belongs to the hospital department. He is, as he deserves to be, very unpopular in the regiment, as he is rough and rude, and seems to care but little about the welfare of the men. I was thoroughly disgusted with him on the 1st inst. at Harper's Ferry. In the name of the Col I requested him to distribute the Hospital stores sent to our Reg from Erie to our sick. He replied that this would be selfish, that he would not do it, but would distribute them to any of the sick of the corps. In the afternoon while visiting the hospitals in company with Mrs. H. Wittich, I met him. He immediately said, "Chaplain! These Hospital stores shall be distributed to the sick of our regiment, for whom they are sent." I said nothing, but curled my lip in contempt. Before Mrs. W the vile hypocrite wanted to seem very much devoted to the duty he owed to our regiment.

I saw Genl Porter review his corps this afternoon. Considerable enthusiasm was manifested. He is to be court martialed, I believe.[9] When we came here, I expected a battle before this. But changing commanders may have delayed it. There are rumors that Lee has already escaped—which would be a great disappointment to us, as it was desired to compel him to give battle in this neighborhood.

It is natural that I should sometimes long to be back in Erie, with my people, again to enjoy their friendship and hospitality—and to impart to their spiritual instruction and consolation. This longing is sometimes a real aching, very akin to homesickness. Deep feelings sometimes overwhelm me, when thoughts of the past, of home, of Erie, of Europe, of sad ties formed but so severed enter my mind then a deep melancholy, somewhat like that which came over me when still a student at Wittenberg College, comes upon me. Then I can only sit and think, or rather feel the past vividly present to my mind, its scenes, its friends and loved ones, its hopes, its fears, it joys, its sorrows, all moving before me as living realities.

Brigadier Gen Hancock, now commanding our Division, however brave and courageous he may be, is addicted to one very unmanly unsoldierly vice—profanity. Day before yesterday he swore most vilely in presence of our regiment. Last evening I wrote him the following, which I have not, however, had the opportunity of sending him, and fear I shall not have.

Camp near Warrenton, Nov[ember] 11th 1862

General Hancock:

Dear Sir:

Finding that profanity prevails to an alarming extent in our midst, I have, as my duty required, attempted to banish it from our regiment. Example in this case, as in every other exerts a great influence, either for good or evil. It is, therefore, with the deepest regret, that I find so many pointing to our Division General as an Example of the grossest profanity. What can my feeble labors accomplish, when in conflict with an example of so high authority, bearing with it such a weight and influence.

I suppose I need scarcely say, that, as you were uttering the most horrid oaths in the presence of our regiment yesterday morning, many of our officers and men were shocked and pained, for we have among us those who regard profanity as low, unmanly and wicked, who reverence the name of God and regard him as the Being who holds their lives, the army, the destiny of our country and the victory or defeat of our arms in his hands; that some looked upon their worthy and so much honored General as giving them a license for their profanity whilst others were in danger of learning profanity from your lips. And it surely is not a pleasant reflection to the soldier, who may at any time, without a moment's warning, be called to meet his God, that the Commander, leading him into battle, dishonors and profanes the name of his God.

I have not written the above, because I forgot my subordinate position, but because I thought it was demanded by my position as a minister of the Gospel, by my duty to our Regiment, to our Country and to our God.

I need not ask you to pardon me for beseeching you to quit swearing; for it is God who commands you: "Thou shalt not take the name of the Lord thy God in vain, for the Lord will not hold him guiltless that taketh his name in vain," and it is Jesus who said; "Swear not at all."

Trusting that you will not regard this beneath your notice and that you will receive it with the same spirit in which it was written,

> I remain, highly esteemed General,
> Your humble and obedient Servant,
> J.H.W. Stuckenberg,
> Chaplain 145th. Regt. Pa. Vols.
> Warrenton Va. Nov 14 1862

(Never sent - from lack of opportunity)

I visited the secesh hospital in the new Bapt[ist] Church yesterday and found about 25 rebels wounded at Bull Run last August. Most of them were wounded in the legs. They have their own surgeon and nurses and seem to be well taken care of. Most of them were from Georgia, a few from S[outh] Carolina, and some from Tennessee and Virginia. They conversed with me freely and gentlemanly, discussing political and martial matters quite freely but not at all with a harsh spirit. They seem to think there is no hope of conquering the South—and that the North will soon give up this war. "Our politicians were the cause of this," said one. They were sincere in their devotion to their cause, believed it right and that God was on their side.

I long for some good books to read, but can get none. I study the Bible daily and enjoy it exceedingly. I have just perused Micah very carefully and have commenced Nahum. The figurative language of the prophets interests me much. I derive great benefit from this study and trust it will bring me nearer God. I long for aids that I may study The Book to better advantage. But the Bible is a rich treasure from which each one can take pure gold without aid from others. My mind is no more as distracted as when I first entered the army. My thoughts seem to flow more naturally again and can be concentrated on a particular subject for a longer time.

I correspond regularly only with my brother and a few Erie friends and at great intervals with my European friends. I correspond with no young lady in whom I am specially interested, and have no special desire to have such a correspondent. I believe that it will be years before love and marriage can be seriously thought of. My plans can, I think, be better carried out as I am, than if I were married. Still I feel most keenly my isolated state. No one on whom to centre my affections, or whose affections I desire to gain, one to live for specially, no one to live for me. I know that my heart was not made for this—it longs too much for deep sympathy, intimate heart and spirit communion, for deep and lasting affection. Ten years ago I did not think I should be now what I am. The imagination, the heart, drew a different picture of life. A family before this age—at least a wife, a home—this was my fond dream. How I longed to be a man just to realize this ideal! Many years, life, may roll away ere I can call one dearly loved one my own. Duty may say 'remain as you are'; Germany may again attract me to its historic scenes and academic halls before a woman attracts me. I may think I can accomplish more in the literary world by remaining single awhile. There is too much reason mingled with my love. I never expect to experience again an overwhelming affection, which hurries one blindly on to its object. The older I grow, the more critical I become, the more difficult I am to please, and the more difficult the choice becomes. Few suit me now that would have done so years ago. Indeed, I have sometimes thought I could by force of will determine never to marry, and have been tempted to do so. But then the youthful and once so much cherished ideal of love, of married bliss would rise before my mind, and the lonely, forsaken figure of an old bachelor would frighten me—and I did not try the power of my will to crush the budding affections of the heart. Could I be really happy for life if unmarried? Could I accomplish more than if married? These and other questions perplex, and I have found no decided answer yet. For me may come another spring of affection, but I think it will not be till the winter of this war is over. Till then—farewell matrimony.

Camp near Falmouth Va opposite Fredericksburg Dec 2, 1862

We left our camp at Warrenton on the morning of 15th ult. and marched some 12 or 13 miles. The next day (Sunday) was the longest march we have had since I am with the regiment about 17 or 18 miles. It would not have been so difficult could we have marched in the road, but as there were four columns marching side by side we could not get the road, but marched through fields and woods over brooks and through mud, up hill and down hill, and got entangled in the brush and briers. I was very tired on Sunday evening.

We encamped in a field about 6 miles from Fredericksburg, beside a clean brook and within a few rods of an excellent spring. As it was Sunday evening I held services in two companies. It threatened to rain and did sprinkle a little during the night. But I slept pretty well—my feet close to a fire my india rubber blanket under and the woolen over me. It was quite cold, but I did not suffer much. Next day we marched within a mile of Falmouth.

Soon after arriving at our camp the firing of artillery was heard—our battery back of Falmouth was shelling the rebels just back of Fredericksburg. All at once the order was given "fall in" and the Irish brigade rushed towards Falmouth on double quick—but the report (that the rebels had abandoned their battery) was a fake one—so we remained where we were. Next morning we went to within sight of Falmouth—expecting a battle the same day, which did not, however take place. We marched from Warrenton to Falmouth in 2 1/2 days—a distance of 40 miles.

Our camp within sight of Falmouth was pretty good with wood and water near; but in order to be out of the reach of the rebel guns we were taken to the top of a hill into a thick forest, where we remained till yesterday morning when we moved to this place, about 1/4 mile distant—for the purpose of going into Winter quarters. Although we are to prepare ourselves for inclement weather I have no idea we shall remain here all winter—at least, I hope not. I want the army to do something.

There were, it's said, but few rebels at Fredericksburg when we first came here; but now they are here in strong force. Their camp fires extend for miles along the river, just back off the neighboring hills. Their pickets are often seen in strong force along the banks of the river. They are busily engaged in throwing up earthworks, as they were determined not to yield their position. A surrender of Fredericksburg was demanded—but, it was not given up. It is a great mystery to us all, why Fredericksburg was not taken as soon as we came—for it seemed to be an easy task then. And it seems strange to us that no active demonstrations are made against it now. We are lying here doing nothing. My opinion is that Burnside[10] wants to hold the rebels here and strike them a blow at some other point.

About two weeks ago Dr. Potter, who seems to delight in speaking about the inefficiency of chaplains had quite a discussion with Lt Col McCreary on the subject. I also joined it against the Doctor, saying that the cant against chaplains was generally made by those least fit to judge in the matter—which incensed him that he was unable to control himself, gnashed his teeth and said: "Chaplain, you do not occupy the position you ought to in the regiment," which incensed all who heard it, condemned it for its personality and falseness. It made me inquire into my position in the eyes of the regiment, when I found that both officers and privates were, generally speaking, great friends of mine. Dr. P[otter]'s very unpopular—he is rude and harsh towards the men; he is proud, overbearing and cannot bear contradiction; and is one of these excitable men who are unable to master themselves. He would be a better Doctor, if he drank less, cared more for the sick and treated them more humanely.

Lt Parker, Co C died at Harper's Ferry on the 23rd ult. We all thought he would recover, but whilst recovering, he took a relapse and died. He was restless and full of anxiety during his sickness. Besides his family, he told me he had an aged grandmother depending on him. He had been a professor of religion but had backslidden, and he seemed to have much anxiety in reference to his spiritual welfare. He asked me to pray for him almost every time I saw him. Once he told me "I am ready to go." It seems he had found peace—and I trust in peace he died.

Many have died since we left Erie, and often has my heart been pained when I saw the strong, healthy and young stricken down with disease and then die—just as they seemed to enter into the prime of life. But no death has affected me so as that of John B. Fickinger. He was a member of our church in Erie, led the choirs till he went to school in Edinboro[11] last Spring. He made up his mind to study for the ministry and expected to enter upon a course of study at Wittenberg college this fall. But the call for 600,000 more men came and he hesitated whether to enter upon his studies at once or to fight for his country first. He chose to do the latter, and about the same time he was to have started to college he enlisted. I regretted it at the time, because I wanted him, being already 22, to enter upon his studies at once. He was stout and healthy and had scarcely ever been sick, and we all thought, if any could endure soldier life, he could. But he began to complain some time before we left H[arpers] Ferry of pain in the back, of general debility—and headache. For a while I took him to Coleman's with me to breakfast, hoping that would strengthen him. He was quite sick when we left the Ferry and could not accompany us. When I returned to the Ferry a few days afterwards I found that he and the other sick had had no medical attendance since we had left. Geo Evans informs me that he wrote home, that after we left the Ferry, Dr. Potter came to his tent and told him to get up and walk out to an ambulance, when he replied that he was too weak and could not do it, when the Dr. replied that if he did not do it "he might lie there till he should rot." He must be a very fiend if he actually said this. John's father came to see him some weeks ago and tried to get a discharge for his son, which object he had about accomplished when John died on the 24th ult. His father took his body home the next day. We all expected him to recover and thought it was a mere question of time. The blow is a severe one to the family, who have but one son and one daughter left.

Most keenly do I feel his loss; not only because he was my member, but because we were so intimate and because I trusted God would have used him in the ministry as a means of great good. But He knows what is best. Our loss is our Brother's gain. Farewell—dear Brother. Thou hast gone before me to our Father's house. To have still held communion with thee would have been a source of joy. But I will try and be resigned. Farewell—but we will meet again. We should not mourn, when such as Thou must die. Still there a pang in the heart, a void left there we fain would have filled; tears will trickle down the cheeks when memory wanders back to what Thou wast and what I hoped of Thee. I will ever cherish Thy memory as dear—and will seek consolation in the thought that we shall meet again at God's right hand.

On the 25th ult. E. C. Sterrett[12] died in the hospital in camp—the fifth death in Co I. He was taken sick (camp fever) about a week before, but was not very sick till within four or five days of his death. On the morning of the 23rd he left his tent soon after midnight and wandered about for some hours as if lost. Sunday Morning (23) he said: "I am sick and shall die within three days," a premonition which seems to have been prophetic. That same morning about 9 he was taken to the hospital, and died Tuesday evening (25th) about 8 and was buried in the Falmouth graveyard the 27th. He was a Christian and has gone home to his reward. He was only about 18.

Second Lieutenant George A. Evans, Company I.

Last Sunday about one P.M., J. Mowry[13] died also of camp fever. He was not a Christian, but during his illness was frequently heard praying the Lords prayer in German. He was about 30 leaves a wife and two children.

Every letter from Erie tells me S. M. Brown is sinking very rapidly and also Mr. S. W. Keefer[14]—and I am urged to apply for a furlough and pay Erie a visit. I made application today for leave of absence for 25 days, and as the result is not yet known I am in great suspense. I wanted to visit our sick about Washington and Harper's Ferry and also look after hospital stores at the latter place, and go to Erie and spend a few weeks there. But I must wait and see what the generals say.

Last Tuesday (27th ult.) was Thanksgiving day, services in the evening at which Rev Wilson Chapl[ain] of 81st Pa made some remarks after which he and his boys sang: "Do they miss me at home" and "Good night." Inspection last Sunday and no services till evening, spoke then with special reference to the death of Lt Parker.

Camp near Falmouth, Va, Dec 10th 1862

Orders to prepare winter quarters were obeyed about a week ago and our officers and men have been busy in cutting logs and putting up log cabins. Many have quite comfortable little houses, plastered and with chimneys, their tents serving as roofs. But as the probability is that we will soon move from here, the labor, most likely, have been in vain. I have heard nothing about my application for leave of absence made about a week ago.

Last week Thomas Acocks[15] of Capt Stiles[16] Co was found dead in his tent one morning. He had apparently been neglected. Saturday 6th evening 11 1/2 Chellis[17] Co B died of camp fever. Sunday 7th Williams of Capt Lynch's[18] Co died in his tent of measles. This afternoon another soldier died in the hospital[19]—making six who have died since we came here. He was buried late this evening for fear we should have no time tomorrow.

My commission came yesterday and today I was mustered in. Three letters from Erie received yesterday all urged me to return. A great battle is expected soon. Snow on the ground—hard frost at night—unable to keep warm towards morning. Preached the funeral sermon of a slave child two years old last Friday. Petition was handed Dr. Potter yesterday signed by all our captains requesting him to resign.

CHAPTER

3

FREDERICKSBURG BATTLE

"It made my heart ache."

December 10-16, 1862

Winter Quarters in Camp near Falmouth Va March 25th, 1863

Whilst being mustered in on the evening of the 10th of Dec last I heard several officers speaking about the prospects of a battle in a few days—greater than Antietam—the greatest of the century. That same evening we received orders to be ready for a march at day break. About 3 or 4 o'clock the next morning the booming of cannon was heard in the direction of Fredericksburg. We left camp about 7 o'clock and halted in the valley to the right of the Phillips house, Genl Sumner's head quarters.[1] There was heavy cannonading all day. I view the scene from a hill immediately in front of Sumner's quarters. Our guns lined the back of the river opposite Fredericksburg and for miles down river.

Attempts were made to lay pontoon bridges to Fr[edricksburg][2]—but the sharpshooters in the city picked off many of our men; the report of their muskets could be distinctly heard whenever the firing of the cannon ceased. Our cannons were fired at the houses in which sharpshooters had taken refuge and from which they were firing at our men. Flash succeeded flash, leaping like lightening from the cannon's mouth, a solid mass of flames, report followed report in quick succession—a number at a time seeming to be simultaneous—a heavy crashing thunder rolling over the valley, and up the hills by which it was flung back in deep reverberations; columns of smoke were seen to rise and bright flames were seen, a number of buildings being on fire. Between three and four o'clock P.M. the firing closed, soldiers were seen hastening on swift horses towards Genl Sumner's headquarters and loud shouts and cheering filled the air—the city was ours. A number of men had crossed in pontoon boats and driven away the rebels.

I hastened back to the regiment just as they were starting. The mail had just been distributed which brought me three letters, one from my mother[3] which was eagerly read and very welcome at such a time, and one from Miss J. H. Clapperton[4] of Edinburgh (containing a likeness) which I could not read before starting—but glanced over as we marched along and one from F. Kleinert of Oldenburg which I reserved for future reading.

Just as we were marching down the hill in front of Sumner's Headquarters—as I folded Miss C[lapperton]'s letter and put it in my pocket—a man was struck by a cannon ball or shell a few rods from me in the arm and wounded severely. Many shells fell among our troops attempting to cross the river, the rebels batteries, which had been silent most of the day, having opened a heavy fire on our troops. We turned to the right and camped for the night, on a hill about 2 miles from our present camp and about a mile this side of the depot. The Col, Lt Col and myself slept together our feet towards and near a large log fire. It was very cold. When we got up the ground was glistening with hoar frost, which sparkled like diamonds in the bright morning sun, and our heads and covering and haversack were covered with it. The passage involuntarily rushed into ones mind: "He giveth snow like wool: he scattereth the hoar frost like ashes."[5]

We were soon on our way to Fredericksburg being about a mile distant. We crossed the upper one of the three pontoon bridges. Walking beside the Colonel's horse at the head of the regiment, as I generally did. I was the 2nd of our regt in Fr[edricksburg] the Col being the first. On the river bank and street we saw many of our troops, abundantly supplied with potatoes, flour, books, tables chairs, mattresses and other furniture and eatables taken from the deserted houses of the city. A soldier gave me two books—"Life of Washington," which I afterwards gave to Col Brown and "Life of Lafayette" still in my possession. Walking down the river bank we saw the havoc made by our guns—walls battered down, houses in ruins, others riddled with balls and all with few exceptions, deserted and carcasses of dogs which had been shot lying in the cellars and streets.

We had gone but a few squares when a shell passed over the center of our regiment, a few feet above us and fell without exploding in the river just beyond us. Our regiment was drawn up in line on the second street from the river in the lower part[6] (down the river) of Fredericksburg. It seems to have been the intention of the generals to give the city for pillage to our soldiers, at least no efforts were made to check them in their work of plunder and of destruction. Stores and private houses were entered by men and officers, and as the citizens had left so precipitately that they could not remove in many cases their most valuable articles many of them secured rich booty. The men groaned under their loads of tobacco which was found in great abundance, and being high in our army, was eagerly seized. Fresh pork, flour, potatoes, lard, rice, beans, molasses were also found in abundance—as well as an occasional duck or chicken. The very finest china ware and silver knives and forks and spoons were also taken—some for use, others as keepsakes. Some very excellent libraries were found from which many books

Fredericksburg Battle

"A street in Fredericksburg, VA., showing the result of the bombardment—Federal soldiers grouped about."

I'm Surrounded by Methodists...

Caroline Street, Fredericksburg.

were taken. Lt. Maury's[7] library was a very large and superior one. I found many of his books and papers scattered about the floor of the outhouse. Furniture was also taken—much too was wantonly destroyed some of the very finest and best. The men lived well better, perhaps, than at any time since they were in service.

The rebels threw an occasional shell into the city, some of which fell and burst quite near us. In the afternoon several pieces of shell fell within a few feet of me. In the evening our reg[iment] was moved farther up the river, but remained on the same street. That night Col Brown, Lt Col McCreary, Lt Grant[8] (acting adjutant till next morning, since which time Lt Black[9] had been acting as such) and myself occupied a commodious and well furnished frame house on the corner (perhaps the S[outh] E[ast] corner) of the street on which the regt was formed. In the opposite corner Capt Reynolds[10] and Lt Clay[11] lodged. We had a good time of it—plenty to eat, plenty to burn (the fire came out of three chimneys of the house, so that Genl French[12] ordered us to put out the fires) and good mattresses to sleep on. We lived again in civilized style, we enjoyed the comforts of home, we gathered around the fire blazing brightly in the hearth and spoke cheerfully about things that were and things to come.

We arose early the next morning—the 13th—so as to be ready for any orders that might be given. After breakfast Capt Reynolds and Lt Clay were with us. It seemed to us that we had never been in better spirits. Our conversation was lively and humorous. Had we but known what was before us! I thought of battle, of wounds of death—and neglected not my Bible nor my prayers. But that the close of the day would find us in such different spirits and our regt in such a different condition—of this we had no idea. It was the morning so bright, so beautiful, so peaceful in nature, of the terrible battle of Fredericksburg. One of those present with us that morning, who was cheerful and happy was to be a corpse before night—Lt Clay—and another one equally happy was to be severely wounded—Col Brown—and all were to be worn and depressed by the awful sights we were to witness.

About 10 A.M. we were formed in line of battle two squares further back from the river, directly in front of the Catholic church, the theatre and Lt Maury's house. Skirmishers were sent out. The shells came sweeping down the streets—one striking a corner house diagonally across from me. I saw distinctly a shell or piece of railroad iron coming down the same street, twirling round and round as it went. When men came to these streets they hurried across them, lest the deathly missiles should strike them. Thicker and faster came the shells, around us was rattling the grape and canister, in front of us was the rattling of musketry constantly becoming quicker and louder. About noon our regiment was ordered on the field. Whilst waiting at the corner of the street to fall into the rear of the regiment many shook my hand heartily, saying "good bye Chaplain!"—the last "goodbye" that some of them uttered. They said it perhaps with pale and trembling lips, and with deep earnestness feeling that they were to pass through a terrible ordeal—their first battle. It almost completely unmannered me—so many thoughts rushing on my mind and deep emotions overwhelming my heart. How many I thought might be killed or wounded—some perhaps of my dearest friends in the regiment, some perhaps, who were not at all prepared to meet their God! But it was a time when calmness was required—and I composed myself.

With our two Doctors I fell in the rear of the regiment. The street that lead us to the battle field presented a fearful sight. It was covered with blankets and overcoats and haversacks and other articles which had been thrown away in the hurry and excitement. Soon we had to pass over a dead body. As we approached the battle field wounded privates and officers met us streaming towards the hospitals, some still able to walk, others led by one or two, others carried—some wounded in the head or breast and holding their hands on the wounds—others in the arms and legs—in every part of the body in fact were wounds to be found. When we had gone a square we came to the edge of the city and Dr. Potter concluded to take a farm house at the corner of the street as a hospital. The regiment went on and left the Dr. and myself there. But it was too dangerous a place for that purpose. Immediately in our front lay the battle field. All around us the shells were flying, falling and bursting, shrieking over our heads, tearing through streets, houses and regiments, scattering their numerous fragments far and wide, and producing the most fearful havoc, demoralization and destruction among our troops. For a moment we stood hesitatingly by this frame house. I was calm—but fully conscious of the danger. I watched the countenance of Dr. Potter—his cheeks were pale, his lips quivering. Men—wounded and frightened—hurried towards and past us

I'm Surrounded by Methodists...

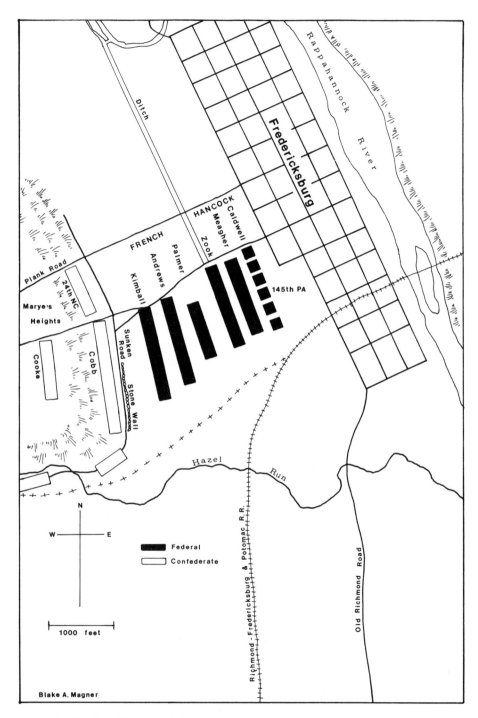

The Battle of Fredericksburg — early afternoon of December 13, 1862.

in the utmost confusion or fell exhausted at our feet. Let men who never saw a battle speak of bravery in battle—they know nothing about it. How a man will feel and act during a battle can only be known after he has been tried. There the stoutest heart may quail and the weakest be nerved with strength and bravery.[13]

To our right I saw a large brick house immediately back of one of our batteries. I pointed it out to the surgeons and we immediately took possession of it as a hospital. I will not—I cannot describe the scene before us—our battery occasionally replying to those of the rebels—just beyond this battery so many of our men wounded and killed by shells, further on still our men drawn up on line of battle firing at the rebels, beyond them the rebels in rifle pits and behind stone walls, and on hills back of them earthworks behind which batteries were planted.

Some of the wounded of our regiment were brought into the parlor of the house we occupied—which was elegantly furnished. The first few were but slightly wounded. Then was brought in one who was still a boy—his name was W[illia]m Wicks,[14] Co D—who was wounded in the groin. He at once recognized me. His groaning was loud and heartrending. "Chaplain" he said, "why don't you kill me? It is cruel to let me suffer so—it is a mercy to kill me." I could hardly stand this—I tried to compose him. Medicine was given to deaden the pain—but it was of little avail. He knew he must die—then came thoughts and fears of eternity—and he spoke to me about his soul. I knelt by his side offered a short prayer and did all to make his suffering less excruciating. He was soon afterwards removed to another hospital—where, I suppose, he died. Pierce[15] of North East was shot through the throat and could not speak a word. Two days later he died and we buried him in Lt Maury's yard.

The Doctors thought it was not safe to remain where we were—so we went with the wounded into the cellar where we found the family of the house and in another room 4 or 5 slaves. Other wounded were now brought in—till all was full. As no more were brought in for some time we dressed their wounds and made them as comfortable as possible. When this was done I went up stairs and had a fine view of the battle. I could see our wounded and dead and our line of battle, before which, from the constant firing, there was a thick cloud of smoke. Many in our line of battle were lying down—loading their guns—they would then jump up, fire and fall down again. I could not see the rebels, but only the smoke of their guns, indeed many who were away in front declared, that they were so well protected that you could seldom see them at all, and then only their heads.

When the work at the hospital was done, I went down to the street where our regiment had been formed in the morning, I found our colors there and perhaps 50 men. I said not a word—but passed from man to man anxious to see who were safe—who missing? Lt Hamlin[16] was the first officer I met. Many a friend then warmly grasped my hand as they came from the field and flocked around the colors. I was particularly anxious about Wm Brown and Dan[ie]l Farver[17]—members of my church in Erie. I soon met the former, but learned nothing of the latter, till I found him in a hospital next day—severely wounded in the ankle, But there was too much work to be looking about.

I found many of our wounded in the streets whom I took or had taken to hospitals; I took possession of several rooms and had them filled with our wounded and taken care of, and some I sent across the river.

It was now dark and I went to General Caldwell's[18] headquarters for permission to go to the field of battle—to assist in bringing off the wounded, but I was told permission could not be granted. So I went from hospital to hospital hunting our wounded and ministering to their wants. The Lt Col was reported wounded—but I saw him about dusk unhurt, I soon found Capts Brown, Lynch and Mason, Col Brown—and a number of our men in the same hospital. At the request of the Col I staid with him till midnight, He was said to be mortally wounded—but has recovered. One ball passed through his right shoulder, another through his right thigh. He was flighty sometimes, calling out in his sleep: "Forward! Rally! That's right!" As soon as he saw me he said: "Chaplain, I am prepared for the worst—if only we had gained the day."

At midnight I went to the house which I slept the nights before. I was so tired that I could scarcely stand. I looked in the room next my bedroom and found the door flat on the floor and just beyond it—an unexploded shell.

A battle is indescribable, but once seen it haunts a man till the day of his death. Even much that might be described will remain unwritten. My conscience was unusually active just about the time the battle commenced—So it was with others. Many entered the battle with a prayer on their lips, others muttering curses. George Demond[19] was brought to our hospital with his left leg shattered—mere shreds of flesh remaining. When he saw me he wept, spoke in German and requested me to write to his wife.

Col Brown was wounded through right shoulder and the right thigh. He was thought mortally wounded at first, but has recovered. 1 Lt Clay, Co A was killed on the field, and his body never found—he was shot through the head. 2 Lt D. Long[20] Co A was wounded through r[ight] shoulder—is recovering. Capt Lynch was wounded in the thigh is recovering. 1 Lt Hubbard[21] was wounded in both legs died—after the amputation of his legs, about a week after the battle. This was the only amputation at which I was ever present. 2 Lt Chas Riblet[22] Co D was missing—we have heard however that he died shortly after the battle from wounds in the breast. 2 Lt Carroll[23] Co E was very lively when brought from the field—then he was very despondent—and died on 16 Dec from inflammation in his wound in the ankle. Like many hundred others he was not properly attended to from the fact that so many, wounded were thrown on the hands of the surgeons at once. A young lady in Erie asked me about him—when I told her of his death she was much affected. Capt W. W. Wood[24] Co G was wounded in left thigh—died in Washington. 2 Lt Vincent[25] Co G—wounded thr[ough] shoulder—died. Capt A. Mason[26] Co H leg amputated—died in Washington. He bore his suffering very patiently. Capt Wash[ington] Brown Co I, Whom I helped recruit his company was wounded in r[ight] arm above elbow. It was bandaged very tightly for 24 hours—and then was not amputated soon enough. He died in hospital near Falmouth. 2 Lt M. Brown Co K lost his leg—was taken to some hospital and not seen by any of our regiment. But his body was afterwards found and taken home.[27]

Fredericksburg Battle

Captain Charles M. Lynch, Company D.

The 14th of Dec was a beautiful day. It was Sunday too, But no day of rest to me. Immediately after breakfast I went on the battle field hoping to identify the bodies of some of our men. It was dangerous, as sharpshooters were picking off all within reach of their guns, so I did not venture very far, but saw enough to shock any feeling being. Bodies were lying about in all directions fearfully mutilated. The wounded were all or nearly all off the field. In a shed on the edge of the battle field I found several wounded whom I had conveyed to hospitals. One afterwards recognized me in a hospital in Washington and was very grateful.

From an elevated position I had a full view of the field. Dead bodies, blankets, overcoats, canteens, arms were scattered about every where. I spied many bodies lying flat on their faces and in rows, which I at first took for dead bodies, but they were our men lying down to avoid being shot. As soon as one arose the rebels fired. One man got up and came toward the city. Instantly a number of guns were fired at him by the rebels—and he fell flat on the ground wounded I supposed; but he jumped up again. As soon as a rebel appeared our men fired at him.

Leaving the field I again went from hospital to hospital, to hunt up our wounded and minister to their wants. In some large hospitals where there were but few nurses, I could not take a step without being called on from all sides to assist some wretched sufferer—some calling for water, for with the wound comes fever, with the fever thirst, some wanting their wounds dressed or moistened to relieve the pain; some desiring to change position, some wishing me to write or speak to their friends. It made my heart ache to see so much intense suffering, crowded in a small compass, and the means to relieve it so totally inadequate. I could not minister to all who desired it, and often had to turn a deaf ear to the most earnest cries for help. This was the most painful of all. I found many of the wounded of our regiment whom I had not before seen, and who were very glad to see me. I had never had any thing to do before this with the wounded; but I soon learned how to handle them, to move them from place to place, to cut off their shoes and socks, to bandage their wounds and make their position comfortable. D. King of Co E had his life saved by a bible over his heart—but afterwards died from another wound.[28] In the afternoon I found D. Farver of my Erie Church—badly wounded in the ankle.

On Monday the 15th I was again occupied with the wounded, who were being taken across the river as fast as possible—and were all removed before evening. It was by no means safe in the city, as the rebels were frequently throwing shells into it, killing and wounding quite a number of our troops. We seemed to be at their mercy—and why they did not throw more shells seems strange. This afternoon, I buried Bryon Pierce of Co C in Lt Maury's yard. Finding Lt Maury's library scattered about in an outhouse, I picked up many of the books and papers and returned them to the box whence they were taken.[29]

Soon after dark we returned to the Falmouth side of the river and went back to our former winter quarters. The evacuation was a complete success. That night Lt Col McCreary, Capt Reynolds, Lt Black (act[ing] Adjutant) and myself slept in a stable, by our present headquarters, covered with pine boughs. It rained very hard during the night, the boughs gathering together the drops let them down on us in streams. I was lying in a kind of hollow, which formed a guttar for the water. My bed was soft, and wet and muddy.

That afternoon, the 16th, word came that Lt Carroll was dying. I hastened with Capt Stultz[30] to the hospitals about 2 miles distant—but he had just expired before we came there. I covered his exposed limbs with his blanket. These hospital tents were on a piece of ground gently sloping towards a creek, with a steep hill on the other side of the tents. From this hill the water flowed into many of the tents the night before, wetting the hay on which the wounded were lying, their blankets and even their limbs. Their covering was in most cases very scanty and the weather cold, this together with the fact that many were lying on wet hay, caused much inflammation, and many died from the effects who, if properly cared for, would have recovered.

CHAPTER

4

CHRISTMAS LEAVE

"The people at home can form no correct idea of a battle."

December 17, 1862 - February 22, 1863

On Wednesday, the 17th of Dec some of the officers urged me to go to Washington with some of our wounded, and see how they were provided for there. I started that afternoon, placed a number in ambulances and went with them to the depot. I tried to get Capt Brown along, but one of the surgeons peremptorily ordered us to take him back to his tent. I worked hard at the depot to get the wounded on the cars, all of which were originally intended for freight and but very few of them were covered. It was very cold and there was much suffering among the wounded. I rode on the top of one of the cars—very cold all the time. At Aquia Creek I helped a wounded man on board of a boat, and staid on it—no questions whatever being asked me, which was very fortunate, as I had no furlough, but only a pass from our surgeon to go to Washington with our wounded. Such a sight as this boat presented! Above and below every nook and corner was crowded with the wounded, so you could only move about with great difficulty if at all, and then some poor fellow would utter some piteous cry because his wounded limb had been accidentally touched. On board I found Capt Wood suffering greatly from his wound.

Early the next morning—the 18th—I helped some of the wounded off the boat and started for the city (Washington) and put up at the "United States Hotel" till afternoon, when I went to a private boarding house. I found Col Brown at Kirkwood House—much better and fast recovering. In his room I met Mrs. Acocks whose son, Company F, I had buried at Falmouth. She had come to Wash[ington] hoping to be able to get his body from Falmouth, but she could get no pass to go there. Poor woman how she planned, and wept and labored for the body of her son!

Washington seemed to be full of hospitals. Churches, public and private buildings being used for that purpose, besides many frame buildings built for hospitals. The battle of Fredericksburg filled these hospitals so full that those who were able were sent to Phil[adelphia], N[ew] York and other cities to make room for the rest of the wounded. In those hospitals you find men suffering from various kinds of diseases and wounded in every part of the body, some slightly, others seriously, some recovering, others sinking rapidly or dying. We had one man there who had 15 wounds received at the Fred[ericksburg] battle, who died from the effects. I found them well taken care of—much better than the sick in camp. They were well provided with clothing, their beds were clean and comfortable, the nurses both male and female, were kind, the physicians attentive. Many visitors came to them and supplied them various articles of clothing et cet. I went from hospital to hospital in Georgetown and Washington, to find the wounded of our regiment and minister to their wants. They had not all been brought up from Falmouth, still I found a great number of them, They were so well taken care of that I could do but little for them. Many sent messages with me to Erie where I expected to go soon.

On Sunday morning, the 21st of Dec I heard Dr. Channing preach in the Senate Chamber, and part of a sermon by Dr. Stocklore in the House of Representatives.[1] The latter looked very venerable and sat in a chair while reading his sermon. I left Washington in the afternoon—expecting to take Mrs. Capt J. W. Walker with me to Erie, but she remained in Washington to await the arrival of her husband, who was expected in a few days.[2] Just before I left, I saw Mr. J. S. Brown, of Erie, who had found the body of his son 2 Lt Co K and was taking it home for burial. He was very desirous of having me preach the funeral sermon in Erie.

I went on the cars to the Relay house that afternoon and left next morning, (22nd) for Harper's Ferry—for the purpose of getting my trunk, left there when our regiment left there, and to see about our sick at that place. I could hear of none of our sick and supposed they were all gone. I had but an hour before the cars left again, and I could only run to Mr. Coleman's, get a few articles from my trunk and run back to the depot—where I arrived just in time to jump on the cars.

Early in the morning of Dec 24th I arrived in Erie. I was heartily welcomed by my congregation and friends. I was frequently stopped on the street, when a crowd would immediately gather around me to learn something of the battle. Many who had friends in the regiment called on, or wrote to me inquiring about those friends. I found many sad and anxious hearts, especially those whose friends were either killed or among the missing. Many questions were, to my great regret, left unanswered.

The people at home, I found, can form no correct idea of a battle and they are therefore continually making wrong representations of it to themselves. They have no idea of the confusion caused by suddenly throwing ten or 12 thousand wounded on the hands of a few, and that as a necessary result some will be neglected, others reported missing. I never had a busier time (except at the battle) than the few weeks I spent in Erie. As for reflection, it was altogether out of the question.

[Note: The following four paragraphs have been moved from slightly later in the narrative.]

Christmas did not seem like Christmas to me. It was a gloomy day, with a drizzling rain. In the morning I had the funeral of Lt Brown, who was buried with military honors. The house was crowded, and many could find no entrance, but stood in the rain. The grief of the family seemed uncontrollable. The circumstances of his death were very sad. No one knew how he died, no friend was near him in his last hours. His body was found in a yard in Fredericksburg with one leg amputated, whilst our men were burying the dead. I also attended the funeral of Capt Wash[ington] Brown, who leaves a wife and infant daughter and large connection to mourn his loss, also that of Robert Finn.[3]

At the earnest request of Dr. Lyon,[4] I agreed to preach in his church on the evening of Sunday Dec 28th in commemoration of those who fell at Fredericksburg. The church was crowded as it had never been before, the gallery, vestibule, choir, ailses *[sic]* all

Private Robert W. Finn, Company D, wounded at Fredericksburg, died in Washington, D.C. on January 3, 1863.

were full, and hundreds went away, unable to get in. I had preached in our church in the morning and had visited Mr. S. M. Brown in the afternoon, and was quite tired; I had had no time for preparation, and was so distracted, confused, and harrassed ever since the battle, that I could have prepared myself but little, even if I had had time. The result was that my effort did not come up to the unreasonable expectations of that vast multitude, which as another said "poured like an avalanche in the church that evening." And for the first time was the criticism in the papers unfavorable. Frequently had my sermons been noticed publicly before this, but always favorably; and it was a real relief for once to find a different sentiment expressed, and the "Gazette" and "Dispatch" afterwards got into a little dispute about the merits of the sermon. I then learned more than ever before, how changeable public opinion and how futile popular applause.[5]

I preached in all my churches and administered in each the sacrament of the Lord's Supper. My presence among my people did much to encourage them. They were assured of my interest in them and had their hopes of my return to them strengthened.

At the urgent request of the Ladies Soldiers' Aid Society—I agreed to deliver a lecture for their benefit on the evening of Jan 6th, my birthday. I had but little time for preparation, and was subjected to constant interruptions so long as I remained in the city. So I went to Mr. Gingrich's[6] and wrote my lecture there. It was an account of my experience with our regiment. It was hastily prepared and mostly written at night. The evening was a very stormy one—and the audience at Farrar Hall was small. The lecture took well and was very credibly spoken of. But the terrible battle of Fred[ericksburg] had made me somewhat indifferent to applause, as well as to censure. Life, I felt was to be made up of something else—of noble godlike deeds and suffering.

[Note: end of transposed section]

I could indeed visit only very few of my members. One of the first I visited was S. M. Brown, who had been suffering for over a year with a cancer, and was evidently near his end. He was one of the Elders of our Church and took a deep interest in her welfare. I valued his counsel highly and knew I could always rely on his hearty cooperation in a good cause. He was also the first delegate I ever took with me from the Erie Church— it was to a conference in New Lebanon, Mercer Co Pa. He had repeatedly expressed the assurance he had that he would see me before his death and before Christmas, and had often spoken about the matter. Indeed it seemed that there was almost something prophetic in it for I saw him the day before Christmas. He was suffering severely. The cancer had eaten away a great part of his neck, and the only wonder was that he could live at all. But he bore his suffering with a patience and resignation, such as I had never before witnessed. Christianity had gained a complete triumph in his heart. He cast his burden in the Lord and felt that He did all things well. It was my custom to close every visit to him with a portion of Scripture and Prayer which he always enjoyed very much, He could only speak in a kind of whisper now, and fearing that it might be difficult for him to converse much, I did not talk much with him. He requested me to administer the Lord's Supper to him the next Sunday—which I did—and also to his wife and daughter Sarah. I saw him as often as I could get time to visit him, and towards the close of my stay in Erie I found him getting weaker fast.

I expected to start from Erie on the 9th of January. But I was very urgently requested to conduct the funeral services of W. Skinner[7] of Co D in Waterford on January 7th. It took me from 6 A.M. till 8 P.M. and thus left me one day to prepare for leaving. As I had a number of baptisms and a multitude of other things to attend to I could not possibly get ready, and therefore concluded to wait till Monday the 12th of Jan.

On the 8th I again visited Brother Brown, and had appointed that day as the one on which I was to pay him a farewell visit; but as I was going to remain longer than I had expected, I said when I left him that day: "I shall see you again next Sabbath." It was indeed my farewell visit, though I knew it not. I was never again to behold that much loved form alive, never again to hear those lips, never again to behold the glance of those eyes, never again to press those hands, never again to say to him: "Brother Brown! Good Bye." I there read to him the scriptures for the last time, knelt down with the family around his bed for the last time offered a fervent prayer with him for the last time. The next day Friday the 9th he died about 4 P.M.—gently sleeping away in Jesus. "So fades a summer cloud away; So sinks the gale when storms are o'er; So gently shuts the eye of day, So dies a wave along the shore."[8]

I did not hear of the death till Saturday morning, and then it filled me with grief. We had all expected his death for some time, and could but look upon it as a relief to him, still when it came, when the bare reality stared us in the face, that he was no more on earth the fountains of grief were opened in our souls, and we mourned and wept. As soon as I could get a conveyance, I went to visit his family, whom I found resigned, but stricken with grief. His long sickness, his intense suffering and excruciating pain had somewhat prepared them for this last stroke. But still the parting was hard—the past with him in it lived before their eyes, the future without him seemed barren of joy. Hope, Hope of meeting him in heaven—this was the most consoling emotion.

The family had been very anxious to have me present in case he should die, to attend his funeral. I had been prevented from leaving on the very day of his death, by another funeral, and it now seemed to us all to have been providential. The funeral took place on Monday the 12th at 10 o'clock. The attendance was very large there being about 100 carriages. The ladies filled the house, so that nearly all of the men were outside. The terrible scenes of war had not so hardened me that I could not feel. Sometimes my emotions threatened to overwhelm me and to interrupt me in my discourse, especially when I addressed myself at the close to the family—of whom only one was absent—W[illia]m—who is in our regiment. The large attendance showed in what esteem he was held by the community. It was, all said, the largest funeral procession they had ever seen. He was universally admired for his sterling worth, his word being as good as his oath.

After the corpse had been let down in the grave, amid the most heart rendering grief of the relatives—I bid the friends farewell. This was the most trying of all. I expected to leave that evening and could not see them again. To part there and under such circumstances was sad indeed and I could not repress the rising emotions and flowing tears.

On the evening of the 12th of Jan I met the building committee of our church at Mr. H. Gingrich's house. A vigorous prosecution of the work of erecting the church building was resolved on. I bid the family of Mr. G[ingrich] an affectionate farewell, and returned to the Keystone House to finish packing my trunk.[9] I had many articles to take to men in our regiment, besides clothing, fruits, cakes, et cet. for myself, given me by my friends. I was accompanied to the depot by Mr. Jareski and Mr. Ruess[10]—and left Erie about midnight. I had the company of Rev Hamilton[11] of Fairview to Harrisburg, and was particularly glad of it at Elmira. Where we had to wait 8 hours.

I arrived in Washington about noon on the 14th and at once commenced the worked [sic] of visiting our sick and wounded in the hospitals and in the convalescent camp. I also attended several sessions of congress during my present as well as my former stay in Washington—and heard part of Bingham's able reply to Valandigham' semi-secesh speech.[12] The latter was moving about among his friends, evidently feeling the stinging remarks and bold charges made against him by his colleague—now reading the paper, then talking to a friend, then interrupting the speaker, his countenance bearing evident marks of disquiet—he seemed occasionally to be cut to the very quick.

The Capital presented many attractions, and I was anxious to hear more of the eloquence displayed in its halls. I attended a lecture at the Smithsonian Institute, but was so tired that I slept during the whole of it—a very unusual occurrence to me.

Wash[ington] is said to be a very wicked place—full of bad men and lewd women—making it; by no means, the most attractive place for a minister of the Gospel.

On Sunday morning the 18th of Jan I started early in the morning for the boat to take me to Aquia Creek. I apprehended some difficultly in getting a pass from the Provost Marshall, because I had no furlough, but I got one without much difficulty. I had some difficulty getting my heavy trunk on and off the boat—but got it through safely. Rev Alvord,[13] Sec[retary] Bost[on] Am[erican] Tr[act] Soc held rel[igious] services on board the boat, which were attentively listened to by the passengers.

I walked from the depot to camp, where I arrived about dusk, much fatigued by carrying a heavy carpet sack, and having a severe headache. I found Mrs. McCreary there who had expected to come with me, but had an opportunity of coming before I did.

Having no tent up, I staid with Capt Hilton a few days. I then put up my tent, but having no means of heating it, I accepted Capt Stultz's kind invitation to lodge with him. In a few days I got Col Brown's stove—and moved into my tent, where I have spent every day and night since that time.

I received a cordial welcome, and no objection was made to my long absence. Many anxious questions were asked about the friends at home and matters in Erie. There was still a deep gloom and depression of spirits in the regiment owing to the late disaster at Fredericksburg. They frequently entertained each other with accounts of what they had done, and seen and heard and felt on that day. Each one had his own tale of doom—and could the experience of any one of them on that 13th day of Dec 1862 be fully given, it would form a most valuable, interesting and instructive account.

I learned that about 500 of our regt entered Fred[ericksburg]; of whom about 450 took part in the battle. We lost in killed and wounded 226 men and besides a number (perhaps 20 or 25) were more or less injured by pieces of shells et cet.[14] Gen Burnside very nobly took the entire responsibility of the battle on himself in a public announcement. His official report is: Killed 1152, wounded about 7000—(figures which seem entirely too low).[15] Genl Lee writing from the field of battle estimates their losses about 1800—but afterwards it turned out to be much greater. Our Corps, the second, lost more than any other and the same is true of our Division.

Since my return I have enjoyed good health, with the exception of a fever, which lasted several days, and which threatened to be camp fever. The weather has been very changeable. On the last 8 weeks, we have been able to hold rel[igious] services only 2 or 3 times; but in the hospital I held services every Sabbath.

[Note: The following entry written on George Washington's birthday is not a part of Stuckenberg's diary; it consists of four manuscript pages located among his other miscellaneous writings. Two of the pages are a theological rebuttal to an article in the *New York Observer* while the final two pages offered a view of camp in the middle of winter. As the passage on camp life logically fits at this point and is not included in the diary, it has been inserted here.]

Near Falmouth Va Feb 22, 1863

This is Sunday and Washington's birthday. When I woke I found the wind strong, shaking my tent to and fro. It was cold too, so that I cannot keep warm in bed with a government blanket, a comforter, a quilt, a shawl—and an overcoat besides over my feet. To keep the wind out I had hung my india rubber blanket before the opening of my tent, but not only the wind came in, but also snow had drifted in and was about 10 inches deep by the opening and extended to my bed and on it half way to my head. The snow without is deep and more still falling. I have moved my table near my stove in order to keep warm—which is no easy matter in so thin a tent, with a good fire even. There is considerable snow inside my tent and more constantly blowing in.

It is such a day as excites the most pity for the poor, the exposed and I often think of those out on picket, compelled to stand in the cold wind and drifting snow, without shelter and without fire, their feet perhaps wet and everything around looking cold and dreary and bleak. Even when not on their posts is the situation any better. They cannot lie down, most probably have no wood for fire and must spend the long night in standing, in walking about to keep warm, in shivering sleeplessness—in contrasting the comforts of home with their present condition. My thin linen tent is but a poor protection against the wind and cold and snow. Even now so near the stove my feet and hands are cold, and the wind comes in strong currents against my head. If at home we saw one living in this style in such weather, how we would pity him! Still we can be hardened to much and the power of suffering and endurance may be greatly cultivated.

I was very desirous of celebrating Washington's birthday with appropriate religious services. I thought of basing my remarks on Ps[alm] 145 4th v[erse]: "One generation shall praise thy works to another, and shall declare thy mighty acts." And what a fine opportunity is presented to the orator here to impress upon his hearers the greatness of Washington, the nobleness of his nature and the immortality of his deeds. We are within sight of the tomb of the Mother that gave him birth. It's on the other side of the Rappahannock but a short distance above Fredericksburg, on a plain running parallel with the river. On a bright morning the white square tops of this monument reflects the rays of the sun so as to render it distinctly visible for a great distance. It is still in the possession of and surrounded by those rebels who are intent on destroying that government and union Washington fought so long, so bravely, so believingly, and under such adverse circumstances, to establish. They desecrate with unhallowed tread the ground that covers her who gave him birth—Mary Washington—the Mother of the Father of his country.

The circumstances in which we are placed are in many respects similar to those in which he was frequently found. We are fighting for our country, our laws and our rights. We have left our homes, our friends—have braved danger, have suffered

Mary Washington's Momument.

hardships and are now exposed to the most inclement weather. Now as then brave hearts beat with hope and fear and anxiety; now as then heroic and noble deeds are done; now as then the fortunes of war are variable—sometimes victory gladdening the national heart, at others defeat filling it with gloom and sadness. Today the Spirit of Washington lives again in our country. The blood-stained hands of rebels have roused it from its slumber. A nation of freemen has risen to vindicate its rights and assert its power. And one looking at us now would see that we are not altogether unworthy of Washington.

About noon the booming of cannon was heard in all directions. The sound was not clear and there was no echo—no doubt owing to the state of the atmosphere. Some reports sounded as if they came from the rebel side and and no doubt was. Would that the name of Washington mutually admired, might form a bond or union between us!

As we have no sheltered place in which to hold services we shall have to do without them today, for we cannot hold them in a storm. No one goes out except when compelled. I have reread some of the old papers and wish I had some new ones. I should like to be with my people today—I always long to be with them on the Sabbath day. For them I offered a fervent prayer to God this morning and hope God will be their Father.

When will the Washington of our crisis appear? One with his piety to God and devotion to country; with his self-sacrifice and heroism; with his skill and wisdom; with his patience and success?

God of Washington be our God! Thou has given us the Father of our country—give us a preserver also.

CHAPTER

5

WINTER CAMP & CHANCELLORSVILLE

"Bright our hopes as that First of May."

March - May 9, 1863

Camp near Falmouth Va Ap[ril] 14, 1863.

The health of our regt has been unusually good. Since 1st of Jan only 2 or 3 having died in camp since that time. Yesterday morning at 11 M. Collom[1] Co B died. He was prepared to go, he said, death would but relieve him of his suffering Disease: Pneumonia. I have visited the hospital frequently distributing the stores sent me by the Ladies of Erie. My relation to the men and officers has been very pleasant. I have their confidence and in many cases their affection. On but a single instance did a man refuse a rel[igious] paper—and he professed to be a blank atheist. I have of late distributed many rel[igious] papers, tracts and books in our regt also in division hospital, in several batteries and ambulance corps and have thus, I believe been the means of doing much good. Last Sabbath I preached my first German sermon in the army to the 127 P[ennsylvania] V[olunteers],[2] and to the same in English. Bro[ther] Ewing[3] of the Christ[ian] Commission preached for me at two.

Last Monday and a week before I attended chaplains meeting at Rev Mr. Alvord's by Stoneman's Station, and found from 15 to 20 chaplains present. The meetings are very interesting. Last Monday (yesterday) I gave my experience as chaplain. I met two other Luth[eran] Chaplains: Shindle and Bro[ther] Saunders—the only Luth[eran] Chapl[ains] I have met. Nor do we know of any more in this army. I am surrounded by Methodist Chaplains, who are very clever, but lack cultivation. They are Chapl[ain] Wilson[4] 81 P[ennsylvania] V[olunteers], Stevens[5] 148 PV, Gregg[6] 127 PV and Conwell (or Connell)[7] 1st Min[nessota].

Last Sund[ay] was a busy day for me—preached at 11 Engl[ish] and Germ[an] in 127 PV. At 1 1/2 held services in hospital around the dying bed of Mr. Collom. At 2 services in camp (Ewing preaching). Visited our hospital again and all the wards of

Div[ision] hosp[ital] with Dr. Ewing. Distributed books and papers in our regt and papers and tracts in our ambulance corps and in a neighboring battery. In the evening Bible class in Co C—Capt Loomis' tent. Held Bible class Tuesd[ay] and Frid[ay] in Co B. On Thursday evening (sometimes on Sunday evening too) prayer meeting in my tent or in Co F—but not regularly. There is little gambling or drunkenness in the regt and profanity has greatly decreased since we entered the field.

About a week ago I bought an 8 years old mare for $70.00—and am much pleased with her—as she is gentle, fast good looking and very easy pacer. Thus far I have always walked, and am pleased with the idea of being able to ride on a march.

The 17th of March was a great day with the Irish brigade—it being St. Patrick's day. It was celebrated with horse and mule races—and other amusements were on the program, but about 2 o'clock firing was heard on our right, and we were all ordered to our quarters and to be ready for a march at a moments notice—for it was said the rebels were coming. Genl Hooker and many other generals were present. It was my first attendance at a race. Hurdles were jumped and also ditches—a break neck operation—many horses falling, instead of jumping, over them—and one man is said to have died from the effects of such a fall. Soon afterwards I witnessed another race—two miles from here—saw horse fall and Col Glam—Glam (I think that is the name) completely stunned and somewhat hurt and another horse turn over its head, apparently on its rider—but both, I think, uninjured. Also saw foot races, race in bags, climbing slippery pole, and men fighting like cocks.

Gen Hooker is very popular already, and a victory or two will make the soldiers enthusiastic admirers of him.[8] Eight days rations were issued this morning and all the surplus baggage of the men was sent to Washington. We are ready for a march and expected orders to start tomorrow, but none has come. Weather is fine, the roads are good, soon the active campaign will begin. Who will live through it? Whom will disease or the bullet hurry to his long home? Thou Knowest.

Camp near Falmouth Apr 17th 1863

Perhaps the reason we are not on a march yet is that it rained very hard all day the 15th. This morning we are to have another inspection (which have been quite frequent of late). On the 14th we were placed in a brigade just formed—commanded by Col Brooks.[9] In Caldwell's Brigade were the following regiments: 81st, 145th, 148th Pa; 7th, 61st, 64th NY and 5th NH. Gen Caldwell is an agreeable man and well liked. There is none of the assumed dignity and importance so common among officers. He is a graduate of Amherst (1855, I believe) and taught an academy in Maine when this war broke out. At college he was regarded as a man of decided ability—and quite witty. He is much more familiar with his officers than General Meagher and is much better liked by them than M[eagher] by his. There is something dashing, spirited, proud and dignified in Gen Meagher. He dresses finely and rides well and the very finest horses. He is calculated to excite admiration, rather than love; and men will obey him because they fear him, rather than because they love him. To me he was always kind.

This camp will long be remembered. We have been in it since the 24th of Nov with the exception of the few days in Fredericksburg. Here we erected our first winter quarters and spent many days in snow and rain and heavy winds and severe cold; from this camp we went into our first battle; to it we returned after the most disastrous failure at Fredericksburg; we entered it, associated in it with many who have gone to their long homes; here we have endured and suffered, a deep despondency here settled on us after the Fred[ericksburg] battle—a feeling akin almost to despair; here we have had joys too, and pleasures; we have been cheerful and hopeful. The five months spent here were eventful ones—and their memory is lastingly engraved on our minds.

Of late cheerfulness has banished the gloom, and hope taken the place of fear. Around Head-quarters we have been quite lively and in good spirits. A pleasant feeling seemed to pervade all, there was peace among us; and many an evening was spent in telling pleasant tales, in cracking jokes or in more serious conversation about home and national affairs. I have spent much of my time in reading and writing, this added much to my contentment in camp. I have some books, besides "The Book"—as Wordsworth's Poems and Tennyson's and part of Byron; also some sermons by Beck (Christl[ich] Sammul[ung] 5tes Heft);[10] some magazines—"Harpers"—; and have regularly received "Luth[eran] Observer," and "Lutheran and Missionary" and (from Miss Olmstead of Erie)[11] "N.Y. Observer" and "Watchman and Reflector;" also the "Kirchenfreund" and occasional papers sent by friends. Besides the above I receive the "Independent"—and consider myself well supplied with reading matter. I have often been in a studious mood and have longed for something more abstract than anything to be had in camp. I have occasionally written an essay—and several times for the papers, besides many letters. For my sermons but little preparation was required and often I could not preach, even when prepared, on account of the weather. I have written three letters for the NY "Herold"—German papers—the first time I attempted to write in German for a paper.

Since my return to camp (from Erie) I have been uniformly cheerful and happy—more so perhaps than at any other period in my life, though I have had seasons when greater and deeper joys were experienced. My trust in God is unwavering; and though I know I am unworthy I feel that in his mercy He will lead me safely and to his glory. My people seem to be more reconciled to my being here, than they were at first, this makes me feel better too.

To the summer campaign which is about to open, I look forward with mingled feeling of pleasure and dread. I prefer to march with its life, its ever changing scenes, its poetry and adventures to the quiet monotony of winter quarters. It will be healthier for us too, I believe. But I know that there will be battles and that some will likely be desperate and bloody. There will therefore be great suffering and much great loss of life. I am so much offended by viewing suffering that it is really painful to me. But still I want to be present at battles, if they must be, in order that I may do all to relieve suffering and point the dying to their God and Savior.

Some 3 or 4 weeks ago I conducted a prayer meeting at Genl Howard's[12] Headquarters on Sunday evening. The sibley tent was full—the Genl and staff and orderlies and others being present. I felt diffident at first, but afterwards felt quite at home. I read part of 6th John and made remarks on it. The Genl's remarks were very good—earnest and practical. "Whenever a friend died, he said the first question he asked himself was whether he had done all he could to save his soul. He had asked himself this question when a few days ago he heard of Genl Sumner's death."[13] It was a good time for all.

Last night I held prayer meeting here. My tent was full of officers and privates. I read part of 8th Rom[ans]. It was a time of real refreshing. My own feelings were deep—I felt concerned for those present because some might never again enjoy such a meeting.

Camp near Falmouth Va May 7th 1863

On the 19th ult. the Paymaster paid our regt to the 1st of March. We have been paid twice and each time on Sunday. On the 21st I went to Washington to express the money for the regt. I carried 92 packages in my Carpet Sack, containing between twenty one and two thousand dollars. It was quite a responsibility and caused me no little anxiety. I stopped at the Kirkwood house.

On Wed[nesday] afternoon, the 22nd I attended the Union Prayer Meeting in Luth[eran] Church, held there regularly since March 1858. Whilst Rev Butler,[14] the Pastor, was speaking in favor of prayer for our country and president two ladies left the house, evidently displeased with his Union sentiments. I had a pleasant visit at his house, where I met Mr. Heyl of Columbia and Rev Burket, and Ebert—Stud[ent of] theol[ogy]. On Friday 24th I returned to camp.

On Monday evening the 27th marching orders, so long expected, came. All were active and busy in making preparations. We were to carry 8 days rations with us. We left camp before daylight to join the rest of the Brigade (Brooke's) on the parade ground. It rained in the afternoon making our camping out unpleasant and roads bad. Lt Col McCreary and myself made a shelter of our oil cloths from which we were, however soon removed, as our regiment were detailed to work on a road several miles distant. After going with the regt a short distance the Adjutant (Lt. Black,) and I returned to our former camp and took a good nap—the more refreshing, because we had slept but little the previous night. We rode through the mud about 2 miles toward evening to join the regt and had scarcely got there when the regt was ordered back to the camp which we had just left. That night for the first time this spring I slept on the ground and in the open air—and that too when every thing was wet and muddy in the forest in which we camped. But I experienced no evil effects as the result.

Next morning we begged some oats from an ambulance driver (of whom we had also obtained some the evening before) for our horses, for which it is not easy to get forage on a march. I discovered to my great regret that my horse had the scratches[15] badly and was apprehensive it might interfere with my progress on the march. In the afternoon we marched at a brisk rate and encamped in a dense forest not far from the United States Ford. About dusk I started to water my horse. After a long search in the woods I found some water. I started back to camp, as I thought, but soon found out to my great astonishment that I was completely lost in that forest so dense that in some places I found it difficult to lead my horse through the low pine trees with their wide spreading branches. It was now quite dark—the denseness of the forest making it much darker than it would have been in an open field. I looked up to learn the points of the compass from the heavens, but not a star was to be seen. The idea of being lost in that country, the thought that I might be compelled to remain there alone all night, that I might come upon some enemies lurking about, all this oppressed me and made me feel very gloomy. I saw before me on the side of a hill just above a ravine a black object which looked I thought like a man. But as I approached it I found it to be a shelter of pine boughs— still looking fresh. Whether made for friend or for I know not. I looked in, expecting to see some one, but saw nothing but black darkness. On and on and on I went, having no idea whither my course would lead me. Finally I saw an opening in the woods and approached it. I came upon a cleared spot, covered with large briar bushes (I think), bearing numerous beautiful white flowers. I passed through them and came to another forest. I halted, hallooed, but received no answer. Back of me some distance I heard the rumbling of wagons and determined to go that way. I turned around, mounted my horse, came to a deserted field in which stood a deserted house, which I recognized as the one I had seen that evening just as we entered the woods to encamp for the night. In a few minutes I was with the regiment again. I felt much relieved, but was tired and the perspiration was rolling down my body. I related my story at "head quarters" and all thought I was fortunate finding my way back to the regiment.

Our camp could scarcely have been a better one. The needles of the pine we strewed thickly on the ground, and the pine trees above and around us seemed to afford considerable shelter. Head quarters were under three or four huge pines, embracing each other, as dear relatives, with their well clad boughs. Five or six forks were thrust into the ground through which poles were laid which were covered with pine boughs, as were also three sides of our quarters for the night. Before us was a bright fire to give us bright light and warmth and add cheerfulness to the scene. This had formerly been cultivated ground, for the tobacco rows were still distinctly visible. The Col, Lt Col, Maj, Adj, and myself slept together that night.

Next morning Ap[ril] 30 the Col learned that he was to have command of the detail which was to lay the pontoon bridges across the Rappahannock—consisting of our own regt and enough men of some others to make 500 in all. The Col was not cheered at the announcement of the honor thus coffered on him, for it made him think of the shells from the rebel batteries and shots of sharp-shooters that might slightly interfere with his operations. But the rebels had left that part of the river and did not disturb us.

It was the day appointed by the President, and on the previous Sabbath I had announced services for that day.[16] But our men worked till near night, and had scarcely rested long enough to cook their coffee when we were ordered off on a march across the pontoons. That night we had a fast and wearisome march till after 10 P.M. when we encamped near a brick house called Chancellorsville.

Next day about noon we heard cannonading and musketry a short distance from us, and it was evident to all that the two armies had met. It was a fine warm day—that first of May 1863. Our army was in good spirits, in good fighting condition, hopeful of success. We had confidence in Genl Hooker's ability as a commander, and were anxious to have our confidence in him confirmed in his first effort to defeat the enemy with the Army of the Potomac. Bright our hopes as that first of May. It has gone our hopes also.

Soon after noon we passed Chancellorsville which was Hooker's Headquarters, and also a hospital. Here two roads crossed at right angles. We turned to the left passed through some woods and came to a house and some fields on our left. We passed the house and in a field our regt were drawn up in line of battle. I saw a number of the wounded coming down the road and in our immediate front, fighting was going on briskly. Two shells passed over me and struck a few rods back of us, but did not explode. We sent our horses to the rear. We entered the woods on top of a hill, posted pickets and sent out skirmishers, all of whom were soon recalled, when we commenced to

Chancellor House. Where Stuckenberg spent the night of May 1, 1863.

retreat. The rebels were after us but I very leisurely fell in behind our regiment and even behind our skirmishers—not knowing to what danger I was thus exposing myself.

We returned to the brick house, but met other troops advancing towards the rebels. We heard the rebels yell like demons—as they rushed upon our troops, who received them with a fearful volley of muskets—which took the yell out of some of them at least. Soon our regt was ordered out again, but was not under fire that afternoon.

In the evening I joined them whilst forming the first line of battle on the left of the road on which we went out towards the enemy in the morning. They were expecting an attack every moment. The rebels could be distinctly heard giving their commands and moving troops—and over the hill a band was heard. Soon the shells came crashing through the woods, some striking and exploding quite near us. Within a few feet of me fell a shell or solid ball which seemed to roll along the ground toward me; when I found it did not explode I went to see what it was, but could see nothing in the darkness. I remained till after the shelling was over, feeling very tired and sick. My horse and blankets were at the place where we camped the night before, but I was so tired that I walked to the brick house, Chancellorsville, borrowed an india rubber blanket and in my thin coat laid down on a board. Till midnight I slept little and suffered much from headache and the cold. At that time Chapl[ain] Stevens of 148th PV came along and took me on his horse to where they had camped the night before, and with him I slept comfortably till morning.

Sat[urday] May 2nd I went to the brick house in the morning and through Lt Col's glass saw rebels at the house on the hill where we had been on Friday morning—and to the right on another hill saw several in a tree apparently making observations. Soon the shells came near the brick house and made the teamsters and others about there hurry away. On the road I found four men gambling, their money by their sides, apparently low, debased characters. The morning before whilst there was fighting and whilst the wounded were coming from the battlefield I saw some drummers between the division Hospital and the battlefield engaged in card playing. Strange that at such a time men can find no nobler employment!

About noon I joined the regiment which had fallen back from the position it held the evening before and was not far from Hooker's Headquarters. They were busy in throwing up entrenchments (at which I had the pleasure of helping them) on front of which trees and brushwood had been thrown, so that it was difficult for the enemy to approach. Whilst there I was rejoiced with the receipt of an excellent present from Miss. Ketchaus—a very fine needle book, which came per mail. I was just reading the letter accompanying it, when the order was given to fall in immediately as an attack was expected. To our right by a plank road, the battle commenced. Volley after volley was fired, grape and canister were poured into the rebel lines. They were repulsed. I viewed the fight from the brick house, the bullets whistling quite near. I returned to the regt where the rebels who seemed to have complete range of our position, shelled us. I was considerably exposed whilst taking my horse to the rear. When near our Division

Winter Camp and Chancellorsville

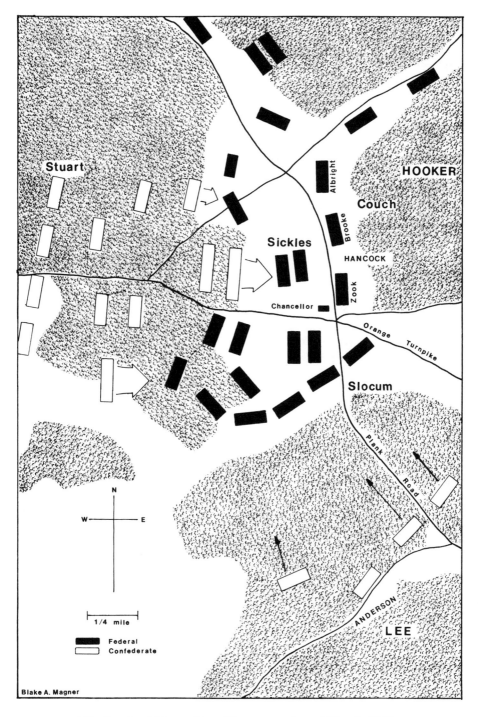

The Battle of Chancellorsville — morning of May 3, 1863.

Hospital, I gave my horse in charge of Farley—colored servant of quartermaster—and watched the stampede caused by the breaking and running of the 11th Corps.

Our right, it seems had been flanked by the rebels. The 11th corps were driven back and were retreating pell mell in the utmost confusion. I saw teamsters and horsemen and infantry by the thousand hurrying away from the scene of action. Some declared the rebels were after them, that we were completely whipped, that the whole army was retreating. I saw a line of calvary with drawn sabres, and beyond them a line of infantry with bayonets fixed trying to keep back the retreating troops—but only with partial success. I thought it looked like a second Bull Run affair. The sight filled me with regret, with indignation and with burning patriotism. The noble cause apparently waning, seemed to me dearer than ever before. I felt as if I could fight for it, die for it, do anything to make it triumphant. Never did I feel more inspired than at that time; there seemed to be within me a burning fire ready to burst forth in the most eloquent utterings. Instead of being borne along with the retreating current, I faced it. They fled from the front, I hurried to it. I tried to encourage and inspire those I met. In going to our regt I met thousands fleeing from the field of battle, but found not a single man going the way I was. No matter, so much greater the necessity that I should go that way. Our regt were glad to see me. I spoke encouragingly to all—telling them the day would be ours yet. All saw I was no coward, and I was highly commended for my conduct. We expected an attack, but it was not made. I staid with the regt that night, I could not leave them at so critical a moment.

About 10 there was another fight that night—terrific cannonading and musketry back of the brick house. I must be near it, so I went to view it from the brick house. The rebels were repulsed. Once more we were disturbed that night by firing in our front, but we were not attacked. I had the pleasure of seeing many of the 11th corps form again in front of the brick house and go on the field of battle again.

On Sunday morning, May 3rd we were aroused from our slumbers by heavy firing on our right about 5 o'clock. The Lt Col took a picket detail of 166 men from our regt besides some men from other regts. He felt that his position would be a very dangerous one, and just before leaving came and expressed his apprehensions to me.[17] About 11 that morning he is supposed to have been captured—for he and Capts Loomis and Oliver,[18] Lts Smart,[19] Devereaux[20] and Stewart[21] and a number of men arc missing, in all 113.[22] He had scarcely left when shells fell into our works and all around us, some quite near me. I then went to view the right, where there was a severe fight. I saw our men marching from the woods—one man firing back just as he came into the open field. Our cannons opened on them with grape and canister and drove them back. Several times whilst dressing wounds near the scene of action the shells came whirling over and around me. I felt quite sick, but did all I could in dressing wounds. One of our men was killed that morning. P. Clark of Co F.[23]

Our regt was taken near the brick house to support a battery. There the Major was wounded and that evening his arm was amputated at the shoulder joint.[24] From this position they (our regt) were repulsed and the whole army fell back. The brick house

Lieutenant Colonel David B. McCreary.

which had been Hooker's headquarters and a hospital was shelled and burned by the rebels.[25] As our troops fell back 3 or 4 or 5 Ladies were seen going through the woods (they came from the brick house) pale and trembling, much exposed to the shells of the rebels. Our front line was now near a frame house in an open field, where new entrenchments were dug by our troops. Genls Couch[26] and Hancock are said to have displayed much bravery and each had a horse shot under him. Genl Hooker is said to have been stunned by a shell.

In the afternoon I saw the woods back of the brick house on fire where there had been such heavy fighting and many of the dead and wounded must have been burnt. The only man whom we know to have been killed was shot this day. The Major was struck on left arm by piece of shell and in the evening it was amputated at the shoulder joint.

As I was going to join the regt I met Mitchell—a friend with whom I had boarded in Davenport and who is now a Lieut (an Engineer) on Hooker's Staff.[27] Such an unexpected meeting at such a place was very agreeable.

I was very weak and also unwell and did not go to the regt that morning. On my way back to Division Hospital I bought a piece of fresh meat with which at noon I regaled myself, two chaplains, 4 voluntary chaplains of the Christian Commission, Lt Mitchell and several others. In the afternoon I went to the regiment, but did not stay long. There was little fighting this day and but few wounded were brought to the hospital.

On Tuesday, May the 5th I felt quite sick and remained in bed till afternoon. It then rained very hard and I had difficulty in keeping myself and blankets dry. In the evening of the fifth orders came for us to fall back across the river. Sad news indeed! We were hoping that we would yet drive the rebels before us. It was a dark, starless night and part of the time it rained quite hard. The mud was deep and pools of water were found everywhere. I was thankful that I had a horse. When I got to the river I found that it had risen so that the pontoon bridges had to be lengthened—so I had to wait quite a while before I could cross. Men were seen shivering, wet and muddy crowding around fires. "You fell did you?" was frequently asked of some who were all mud. "Yes, not once but a dozen times" was the reply. It was midnight when I crossed. The roads from the river were so blocked with cannons and ambulances that I waited after crossing about an hour, and then found a path up a very steep hill which I tried to ascend leading my horse. Half way up in the steepest place, my saddle and blankets and all slipped off the horse and fell in the mud. But I managed finally to get to the top and with a number of others belonging to our regt camped in a pine grove, thankful for a shelter tent which Sam Weidler[28] allowed me to share with him. My feet and pants and blanket were wet but never the less I slept soundly till daylight.

Wed[nesday] Morning May 6th was still cloudy and rainy. Troops were constantly crossing the bridges. Many of them had not rested all night. I had not a morsel to eat, so I obtained coffee and hard tack from my companions. As they left our night quarters a few minutes before I did, I immediately lost sight of them. I found that our corps was on ahead and rode on briskly to catch up with our regt. Our troops looked worn and fatigued, wet, and cold, and muddy. They no longer heeded the mud but carelessly waded through it and water. They thought it made but little difference as they could not be more wet and muddy. Still they appeared to be in pretty good spirits, though this retreat somewhat discouraged them. One of our Lieuts told me he had seen the tears trickle down Genl Couch's cheeks as he crossed the bridge. It was not long before I found the regt. They had formed the rear guard of the corps and had been in the rain and mud all night without rest or sleep or opportunity even to make some coffee. Some were on the point of giving out and laid down in the mud to rest. They had left the front at 4 that morning and at 3 P.M. we arrived at our old camp—11 hours marching in the mud and water and rain.

May 9th.

And now we are back again in our old camp, which we left twice for the field of battle, and to which we twice returned, our numbers each time greatly diminished. I have felt somewhat lonly and homesick since my return—and sad because I miss the presence of so many, especially of our Lt Col. For more than a week I have seen no daily paper and consequently [know] but little about operations in other parts of our country. The result of our battle at Chancellorsville I have not yet learned. The day after we returned to camp, orders came that we should be ready for action by noon of that day. But we are still here. There is but little evidence of spring yet. The nights especially are quite cold, and buds have scarcely made their appearance.

When will the horrors of this war close? When can I again be with my people and friends? Oh I am so anxious to be back in Erie with my dear people. They are working on the new church, the frame is up and their hearts yearn for my return. But I believe it still my duty to stay with the regiment, where my efforts for good have not been in vain.

The First English Evangelical Lutheran Church, Erie. Built in 1862.

CHAPTER

6

CHASING THE ARMY OF NORTHERN VIRGINIA

"The hardest week's march we ever made."

May 24 - July 1, 1863

Camp near Warrenton Junction Va July 29

I sent the Journal, which I commenced when I joined the Regiment and kept till my last visit to Erie, to my Brother[1] in Cincinnati. I have kept no journal since then, for so active has been the campaign that I had but little time, disposition or opportunity to write.

On the 24th of May, I started for Erie on a ten days furlough, and went by way of Baltimore and Ohio RR. In many places the scenery was grand and romantic. The rebels had made a raid a short time before and destroyed part of the track. I arrived in Erie the 26th 1:30 P.M. and was cordially received by my numerous friends. I expected to be in Erie the previous Sunday, and Mrs. Keefer[2] had actually expected me at that time. She seemed to have a kind of presentiment that I was coming.

I was very busy all the time I was there—about a week. I found the church building progressing finely, Mr. Ruess just putting on the roof. On Monday, June 1st we had a Picnic in Cochran's woods, of Sunday School Church and Friends, gotten up for me. For about an hour before assembling and an hour after assembling in the woods it rained very hard, drenching us completely. In the afternoon I gave an account of the battle of Chancellorsville and said some pretty hard things against the "Copperheads,"[3] thereby offending quite a number of my members, who afterwards treated me coldly, and manifested their displeasure. I heard that it was reported by some that in camp I was in the habit of drinking, a most malicious falsehood, as every one in the regt knows.

My members urged me to return to my charge as soon as possible, a request with which I want to comply as soon as possible. On the 30th of May Lt Col McCreary returned from Richmond—an exchanged prisoner. He was in good spirits and met with a hearty reception. I took Miss S. L. Olmstead to a concert—which of course occasioned Some talk and some I heard that I was engaged to her.

On Thursday June 4th I joined the regiment. The next day on dress parade Col Brown in behalf of the regiment presented me with $115 "as a slight token of their regard" as he said, for the purpose of purchasing a horse. The matter had been talked of before the Chancellorsville battle. But after the regiment was so reduced (having little over 200 men) that I thought it would not be done. The officers gave $55.75, the men gave the rest. I value the gift on its own account, but more because of the feeling it indicated.[4] On the 8th of July I bought a bay mare, five years old, of Mr. Danner near Frederick, Md for $150 horses being very high. This token of their appreciation and regard makes me feel less like resigning as chaplain. I have had many evidences of the kind feeling the regiment cherished towards me, and thank God that He has answered my daily prayers—"to bless me in my labors in behalf of the regiment".

The regiment were paid just before my return. I procured a pass 10th of June to Aquia Creek for the purpose of expressing the money, and managed to go to Washington—walked about till pretty late in the evening and started for the regiment next morning.

We expected another campaign to commence soon as Lee was in Maryland and Pennsylvania, and looked daily for marching orders. They came Saturday evening June 13th. We packed up during the night, sent off baggage at daylight and were ready at the time to start ourselves. Whilst waiting to start, I reflected on "Life in Camp near Falmouth" of the joys and sorrows there experienced, the hardships and dangers through which we had passed, the friends and comrades who came there with us never to return—all passed like a panorama before my eyes.

In the afternoon of Sunday June 14 we (our Brigade) bid farewell to camp, started on our retrograde march bringing up the rear of the army. We went to Banks Ford, halted about 15 minutes, then marched again till late at night we bivouacked, weary and sleepy, in front of Berea (or Hartwood) church.[5] Knowing that we might be attacked we threw out a strong picket. It was a restless night for we were several times aroused.

We were on the march again early in the morning. Col Brown having been appointed Corps Officer of the day, on the 14 was not with us, so Capt Reynolds had command of the regt. Having the use of Lt Col McCreary's horse I got along very well. The day was intensely hot and close. We marched very rapidly, to join Division, and escape the enemy who might be pursuing us. Before we arrived at Stafford CH, which we did about 10 A.M., we found trees had been felled across the road, to prevent the enemies calvary from attacking the troops at the C[ourt] H[ouse], and we afterwards learned that Genl Hancock supposed that perhaps we had been captured. For two hours we lay in the dust at Stafford CH exposed to the burning rays of the sun. I felt quite sick, sleepy and tired—and slept in the sun. My head felt dizzy—it seemed as if I was

Captain John W. Reynolds

going to be very sick. The march was resumed about noon. Good water was very scarce. The heat was almost intolerable. The road was lined with those that fell out panting and exhausted. Many cases of sunstroke occurred. That night we bivouacked near Aquia creek where we arrived in the afternoon. The guns were scarcely stacked, before all the men and officers were asleep on the ground (Dumfries—old grave yard). I never saw men more tired. Sick, sleepy and weary as I was I felt more for the men who had to walk and carry heavy loads besides. It was such a march which men say they dread more than a battle.

On the morning of the 16th we were ready by daybreak to march, but were delayed an hour or two. It was not quite as hot as the day previous, but many fell out—still feeling the effects of the march on the 15th. I did all to help the boys along, carried their guns for them and let them ride my horse whilst I walked. It was very dusty too, so much so that at times we could scarcely see the men immediately in front of us. Great clouds of dust rose around us—I thought one might write in them, they were so thick.[6] We crossed Occoquan Creek after dark and bivouacked on its northern bank for the night.

It was very hot again next morning. About noon we arrived at Fairfax Station and pitched tents. I just gave out. We remained here till the afternoon of the 19th when we again struck tents and marched to Centerville where we arrived about dark. Before our tents were pitched it rained very hard wetting me to the skin.

On the morning of the 20th I went to the village, which at one time contained perhaps 400 inhabitants, but is now little better than a mass of ruins. There were about 4,000 troops there of Heintzelman's Corps,[7] some of whom ached to get into a fight. Centerville lies on a high hill from which the view is very extensive, varied and grand. The small white frame house which formed Gen Kearney's Headquarters just before his death stands on the side of the hill and Chantilly where he was killed is but a few miles distant.[8] Far away in the distance the mist-covered summit of Bull Run Mountains is seen. After the first Bull Run battle our army retreated over the hill towards Washington. I felt that I was standing on historic ground, that all around me great events had transpired which had rendered immortal names before unknown.

The troops at Centerville looked as if they had not seen any hard service, and were called by our soldiers "band box soldiers". Their fare was good and also their clothing, their duties were light compared with ours; and all had wedge or wall tents; the country was beautiful and constant communication was held with Washington, which is only about 25 miles distant. Still they seemed to be discontented.

We left Centerville about noon of Saturday 20th on what was called a forced march—very much forced, we thought, before it ended. About 3 miles from C[enterville] we crossed Cub Run after which we entered a large field on which graves were seen and on trees and stumps bullet marks, it was Bull Run Battle field. Solid shot, pieces of guns, of shells, of wagons were scattered about. Here it was that on the 21st of July 1861 the Union troops and rebels met in force for the first time. That battle, so important at the time, has since been eclipsed by others far more important and bloody. The main part of the battle field evidently lay to our left. The remains of winter quarters used by rebels were seen on our right—good, substantial log huts, covered with oak boards. After crossing Bull Run creek we came to the second Bull Run battle field. The stream was at that time about two rods wide and a foot deep. On the battle field is a village of 3 or 4 houses (called Grovetown)[9] over one of whose doors a solid shot or shell entered the house. Before Grovetown we halted for a rest. To our left were seen numerous elevations in which I at first supposed horses were buried. But on closer inspection I found that human bodies had been interred. Graves had not been dug, but from either side a little earth had been thrown on the bodies, barely sufficient to cover them. The rain had in many places washed away the earth, exposing the skulls and other bones of the bodies also remains of clothing—the blue pants and coats indicating that Union soldiers were buried there. By our regiment, separated from all the other bones, lay a skull which was freely handled by our men. I never before knew what was meant by "the bones bleaching on the field of battle". It was a horrid, ghastly sight. "The worst we have yet seen," said an officer. One could not help thinking that a similar fate might be his; that some day his bones might bleach on some Southern field and be carelessly kicked about, no board to indicate their owners name. We turned away disgusted with the sights. We had been hardened by battles and scenes of horror, but could not view such a scene without a shudder.

At Gainesville we struck the rail road. As it was near night and all were tired it was supposed we would bivouac there. But we were disappointed. About a mile from G[ainesville] we came to what had once been Haymarket, but Sigel[10] is said to have destroyed it. Nothing was left but the chimneys, the houses had been burned. Night came, dark and dreary, but still we marched on. We were tired, roads bad, still we marched on rapidly and without rest, till about nine P.M. we bivouacked at Thoroughfare Gap. The men were too tired to make coffee, though some had not had any since morning. Thus ended a week of weary marching in hot weather and over dusty roads. It was the hardest week's march we had ever made. It seemed as if we had been from Falmouth two or three weeks instead of one. Sometimes it seemed as if the sun could scarcely shine any hotter on the great Sahara, and as if a simoon[11] could not raise thicker clouds of dust than we encountered just before crossing the Occoquan. Such marches are well calculated to prepare a man for traveling in Africa or some other hot climate where water is scarce.

Sunday morning June 21st was bright and warm. Capt Reynolds took a walk with me into Thoroughfare Gap.[12] I was just in the mood for enjoying the scenery, so wild, so beautiful, so romantic, forming a sublimity and grandeur seldom seen. From the flat on which our camp was located we ascended the embankment on which laid the railroad track. Walking a short distance on this track we entered a pass in the mountains which rose abruptly on our right and left and were covered with heavy trees and a thick under growth, forming a closely netted verdure. The vegetation—herbs, shrubs, grasses—is luxuriant, and in many places so closely matted as to hide the earth whence they spring. The Gap seems to have been made for the sake of Broad Run, over whose bed of gravel and broken fragments of rocks the crystal stream flows or either falls with ceaseless melody. The same constant flow and sound might become monotonous were it not for the reflection of life and love and joy awakened by the living stream meandering its way through huge mountains. On many spots it is hid by overhanging bushes and variegated flowers, and only know it is there by it's deep guttural voice.

At the entrance of the Gap on the left were a number of burnt posts, on which had once stood a slaughter house; farther on was the deserted depot, a little farther still a large, substantial building—walls 3 feet thick, and a wheel 30 ft in diameter which had been a mill. On the right, the miller formerly lived in a large stone house, built in 1812 in a beautiful spot. It had evidently been the home of wealth, but it looked neglected and dilapidated now. A shell had struck the wall and entered the cellar last summer. Back of the house was a deep hole, which had been an ice cellar, and farther back was the family burying ground, in which lay the remains of the former resident and family.

Farther in the Gap to the right stood another mill with its two wheels, its broken and moss-covered boards and time worn foundation and sides and roof, looking in its ruined state and deserted condition as if it belonged to the ages of antiquity. Farther on still the side of the mountain on our right rose very abruptly, being one solid mass of rugged jagged rocks. Altogether the scene was majestic. There was little life there, but every thing suggested and awakened the highest types of life and character. Such scenes filled ones mind with grand ideas and always create in me a desire to travel and see the wildest and most majestic scenes in nature. Some views are so extensive and complicated that they cannot be fully comprehended, filling the soul with mystery and awe, which was the case in Thoroughfare Gap. A fine spot this, thought I while gazing

"Thoroughfare Gap, Va. A pass in the mountains on the Manassas Gap Railroad."

at the old mill, today the scene of some novel or romantic story. We repeatedly visited the Gap, always admiring and wondering; this same Sunday evening in our desire to see all, passing unconsciously beyond the picket line.

This Sunday morning, which did not seem like Sunday, we returned to camp just in time to move about 1/2 mile with the regiment to guard the road on the side of Bull Run mountain. There are days in our history when all the fountains of feeling are opened, days of peculiar tenderness, when a bird or leaf, or brook, or landscape, or look, or word unlocks to memory the storehouse of the past and sends the soul in keen hopeful fearful longings in the future. We think and feel, we remember and long feel the poverty of language to express our ideas,—they are themselves perhaps vague and unidentified as the feelings whence they spring on with which they are connected. Love reigns then and for absent friends and the loved of former days we feel a regard peculiarly tender— former affections are revived. We clothe every object in the light of our own feelings. Such a day was the first Sabbath spent on our last camp near Falmouth and such a day was the Sabbath spent at Th[oroughfare] Gap. A melancholy, similar to that so common during my college days, then comes over me. Our walk in the evening was in the moonlight, the gloom hanging over the stream and rocks and forests and mountains adding to solemnity of the grandeur.

We remained at the Gap till Thursday morning June 25th. Cherries were abundant and the first few days we had as many as we could eat. Several days I spent in studying botany in which I became much interested. Besides learning many new facts and terms, my attention was directed to plants as it never had been before. One evening I held a Bible class by the side of the road, which was well attended. I spent my time pleasantly and profitably, in viewing the scenery, in reading, writing and meditation.

Early on the morning of the 25th firing was heard to the east of the Gap not far from us. We were soon ready to march and were hurried away rapidly. We had gone but a short distance when we halted and the order was given to load, when I saw 3 or 4 horsemen riding to the edge of the woods a short distance in front of us who on seeing us, immediately turned back into the woods. They were no doubt rebel cavalry. Skirmishers were kept on both sides of our columns all morning.

Instead of returning the way we came, we turned to the left just before reaching Haymarket, and soon after heard cannonading in our rear, which was attacked by the rebels, and who wounded a number of our men. About the same time our regiment was ordered back about a mile or two over the same road just passed over, to guard a road running at right angles to the one on which we were traveling against any attack from rebel cavalry. Every moment we expected them. At one time a number of cavalrymen came from the woods, but they happened to be our own. I remained with the regiment while there.

It was a hard march we made that day, with little rest, and all were glad to camp at Gum Springs in the evening. It was dark when we got there, and with difficulty we put up our tents, first removing leaves and rubbish. It was not a very clean place, for soldiers had before this camped near there. It rained hard in the evening and during the night. Though the shelter tent occupied by Capt Reynolds offered but little comfort in the rain, and though completely drenched with rain during the march, I slept soundly in my wet clothes.

On Friday June the 26th our march was not so severe. About noon we halted on the southern bank of the Potomac, and beheld with pleasure the shore of Maryland. We wanted to leave Virginia, had found ourselves in it unwelcome guests wherever we went. We crossed one of the pontoon bridges at Edwards Ferry, after dark, marched several miles over bad road and after midnight between 1 and 2 o'clock we rested our weary limbs in the edge of a fine grove.

The next day Saturday June 27th we again marched till near midnight and bivouacked beyond Barnesville. We everywhere saw indications that we had left Virginia—in the villages, farm houses, farms and people. The latter gave us a cordial welcome and treated us as friends—so different from what we had been accustomed to in Virginia.

On Sunday the 28th we were roused early and marched over Sugar-loaf mountain and soon saw the rich and beautiful valley in which Frederick City lies stretching out before us. We struck the Monocacy about noon and pitched tents. After washing in the river Capt Reynolds and I went to F[redrick] city—three miles distant. It is a beautiful city of about 8000 inhabitants. Many of its residences are large and beautiful; its convent is quite large. The Lutheran church is very prosperous in this region, the congregation being the largest in the city.

Whilst riding through the streets and viewing the apparent prosperity of the city, the ease and comfort of the citizens and the clean, well dressed and beautiful children. I could not suppress a feeling of sadness and tears filled my eyes, because these scenes brought vividly before my mind what I had enjoyed and was now deprived of. Many flags were displayed in the city a truly cheering sight. From not a single house in Virginia had we seen our country's glorious banner displayed.

There were many soldiers in town and some of the streets were crowded with teams. It was indeed sad to see so many soldiers staggering or lying about the pavement dead drunk. One man hanging on an iron fence called us piteously for help. One of his hands was between the sharp iron points and his leg. Several holes were actually pierced through his bleeding hand and his leg had no doubt been penetrated by the iron.

We called at Dr. Geo Diehl's[13] house, but did not find him in. Called again and took tea with Dr. D[iehl] and wife, Capt Stork (son of Dr. Stork[14] of Baltimore) and an Episcopalian chaplain. Mrs. Diehl was full of life and talk and as patriotic as talkative. Her language was very spirited, she was much animated when speaking of the rebellion. Our visit there was quite pleasant.

There was only one church open in the evening—the Methodist—so we went there, but found only the two preachers and about 15 soldiers present and not one citizen. An opportunity being given for any one to lead in prayer, I embraced it. After short services there we called on Rev N. L. Harrison an old college friend of mine, who received us very cordially. Whilst at Frederick, we learned that Hooker had been superseded by

Meade.[15] To many, who had lost confidence in Hooker, this announcement was received with joy. But I felt sad that a change should be made when so near the enemy. I had learned to admire Hooker, notwithstanding his failure at Chancellorsville. But all regrets were vain.

On Monday morning June 29th I carried the mail to F[redrick] and visited a number of young ladies with Rev Harrison, and heard some very good music. About noon I left F[redrick] and hurried forward toward Uniontown to join the regiment which had started early in the morning. After 3 or 4 hours I came up with them. They had marched rapidly and looked very tired. Soon after dark we came to a village called Uniontown, where Lt Mitchell was looking for me and persuaded me to accompany him to the house of Rev Miller, where I met Dr. J. J. Weaver—a Lutheran—who invited me to stay at his house—which I gladly did. Before entering the village Lt H. Lewis[16] came weeping to the rear of the regiment said he could go no further, but had never fallen out, and did not want to do so now. Dr. Richards[17] was riding my horse at the time. I requested him to let Lt L[ewis] ride my horse—which he did—thus keeping him up with the regiment. Next morning Gen Hancock complimented us highly for our march the preceding day of 30 miles.

Our men were completely worn out and they needed all the 30th for rest. Not being very well I remained at the house of Dr. W[eaver] where I was very kindly treated. My stay at his house formed to me an oasis in the desert of this war. I fared very well, had good meals, slept on a soft bed and lived in civilized style.

On the 1st of July we left Uniontown, marched through Taneytown, where I called on Rev Williams[18] of our church, looked anxiously forward to our entering our own beloved state—Pennsylvania—crossed the line with much pleasure, heard reports of an engagement at Gettysburg and of the death of Gen Reynolds[19] whose body was conveyed past us in an ambulance, and after dark moved into a wheat field threw out a picket as we did not know, but what the enemy were in front of us, and bivouacked—glad once more to rest our weary limbs.

CHAPTER

7

GETTYSBURG

"Farewell Brother, we shall meet again."

July 2 - 6, 1863

On the morning of July 2nd we were up and off early—marching towards Gettysburg, which was only 2 or 3 miles distant from camp. Turning to the right we halted in the woods. The occasional firing near us assured us that another battle was imminent. Col Brooke summoned all the officers of the Brigade before him, and said that Gen Meade had requested all the Commanders to exhort those under them to do their duty faithfully, and that here perhaps the impending battle might end the war. Col Brown also exhorted the regt to do their duty.

We were soon marched back across the Taneytown road, and the brigade were massed in columns by regts. Our corps formed part of the centre of the line of battle, being to the left of the cemetery. Skirmishing was going on briskly in our front. We could see skirmishers firing, advancing and falling back. A general engagement was every moment expected. Seeing the Irish brigade bowed in prayer and feeling deeply impressed with the idea that many might enter the battle never to return, I asked permission of Col Brown to hold worship before entering the battle. He willingly acquiesced. "Attention" was called. After a few remarks we joined in prayer. The occasion was a very solemn one—it was the last prayer in which some of our regt joined.[1]

I lay with the regt till about noon, when becoming hungry, I started to hunt my horse which had been sent to the rear with my provisions. After hunting for more than an hour in the hot sun I found our Division Hospital in the woods and my horse near it. I was very tired and after dinner lay down to rest. But immediately the heavy thunder of cannon was heard on the front. This was about 3 P.M. I jumped up, took my canteen and some bandages and hastened to go to the regiment. But coming to the top of a hill the shells fell rapidly between the regt and myself, and I thought it folly to expose myself.

I remained on this hill for a while, attending to some wounded men, watching the prisoners who came in and the fight generally as much as possible. But soon my position became too much exposed. The shells came nearer and nearer, some exploding just in front of me, others passing over my head and pieces falling far and near around me. One struck the ground a short distance before me and threw its pieces and earth and rocks high in the air. Some shells fell near the place where my horse was. A kind of panic seized the "bummers" and others all of whom hurried farther back. The hospital was moved hastily. I moved my horse, took him farther back to the side of a hill under cover of some high rocks. Leaving my horse there in charge of some of our regt. I went to assist the wounded.

Our hospital was at the foot of the hill. Going towards it, the first one of the first wounded men I saw was Col Brown, wounded in the right arm above the elbow. I led his horse to the hospital, where his wound was examined and the cheerful announcement was made that his arm need not be amputated. As Dr. Potter put his fingers in the wound to discover the extent of the injury, Col B[rown] was writhing in pain—his sufferings evidently being intense. About the same time Col Zook[2] was carried to the hospital on a stretcher, mortally wounded.

Col Brown requested me to hunt the Adjutant who was very badly wounded. I at once started towards the field of battle. At the 11th Corps hospital[3] I found Adj Black wounded through the breast, mortally Dr. Whillden[4] thought. He looked very feeble, said little and that in a voice scarcely audible. He thought himself that he could scarcely live till morning, said he suffered greatly, was willing and ready to die and longing for death to relieve him. I asked him whether he had any words for his parents? "Tell them," he replied "that I fell in a noble cause." "I have been a bad boy," he said "but God is merciful." He was calm and seemed perfectly resigned to his fate. Some effects about his person and his sword he requested me to send home to his parents.

I also saw Capt Reynolds at this hospital, wounded on the left side of the head. He was much excited—elated because our regt had done so well and had driven the rebels before them. I found many more here of the wounded of our regt. As many as could be easily be moved I directed to be taken to our corps hospital, others were made as comfortable as possible.

I left this hospital and with Dr. Richards started for the battle field where our regt had fought, hoping to find some of our wounded. We met a number of regts leaving the field and saw two guns drawn off by hand. It was dark and the road was not very good.

We soon came to a house full of wounded men, with only one or two well ones to wait on them. We went on farther, over fields and rocks and stone walls and through woods not knowing whither our course would lead us. We met few soldiers, heard but little noise. The very stillness was fearful and oppressive. A dread came upon as I neared the ground where the desperate fighting had taken place in the afternoon. At any moment I might stumble on some corpse or fall over some wounded man. We frequently stopped to listen for groans, but heard none till we came to another house.

I asked for the wounded of our regt and found one man answering to my call. I passed through between the wounded men outside the house, entered the house, with difficulty passed in the dark through a room in which were some wounded men, and entered another room. On a bed suffering terribly lay Forbes of Company G,[5] wounded through the breast. He begged us to dress his wounds, but as there was no candle to be had, this was out of the question. I gave him some whiskey to stimulate him and then left him promising if possible to have him removed to our Hospital, where I had the pleasure of seeing him the next morning.

I left the many wounded at their house (no physicians to attend to them, no candle even, though they were taken away as fast as the ambulances could carry them) and went further to the front. Back of the house we saw the first corpse. Scarcely had we passed it when a bullet from the rebels whistled past us and warned us to proceed no further. Nor could we have gone much further, for our picket line was but a short distance in front of us. In again passing the house we had just left we heard subdued, but constant groaning near the barn. I found a rebel there, seriously wounded, who gave no answer to the question, whether I could do anything for him? he being perhaps unconscious and near his end.

In passing from the field we learned that a wounded man was lying all alone in the woods. We carried him to a place where he could easily be found, and sent a stretcher for him. We went back to the hospital, where I found quite a number of our wounded. I then went to bed. Seldom had I been so tired. Nature had endured all it could and now coveted the balmy restorer—sleep.

In visiting the hospital on the morning of the third I found the surgeons and nurses busily engaged with the wounded, scattered around in all directions, some lying on blankets, some on straw, a few on stretchers, others on the bare ground. E. Allen[6] of Co G, shot through abdomen suffered terribly. Some of the intestines protruded through the wound and some of their contents would occasionally flow out, producing a horrible stench. Adj Black was much easier and looked much better. The Col was walking about, doing well, he started for Baltimore this day. It was very evident that our regiment had again suffered severely, though the extent of our loss was not yet known—many of our men wounded being still missing.

I soon started to the front to see the regt. It was very small—66 men and officers, commanded by Capt Oliver. Though saddened by their heavy loss, they were in good spirits because they had driven the rebels and taken 75 or 100 prisoners. It was evident that another engagement would take place that day. I was not well, had not been for some days. I withdrew to the neighborhood of our Hospital and tried to sleep. But soon our right, immediately in front of me, was heavily engaged by Ewell's corps, formerly Jackson's. Our right was held by the 12 corps, commanded by Slocum.[7] On the evening of the 2nd, one Brigade of 12 Corps were left to defend the rifle pits on our right, which were driven back by Ewell's men, they thus gaining our pits.

On our extreme right were three batteries, each one occupying a commanding position, which were almost incessantly throwing shells at the rebels. The rebels had fired no cannon at our right. I ascended a rocky hill—it was composed of large masses of rocks—to the middle one of the three batteries. Gen Slocum was here, in person directing the firing. A short distance before us was a round hill, covered with trees. On the side of the hill nearest us, the smoke was seen rising in columns from the forest— there the fighting took place. The rattling of musketry was constant, rapid and terrific. The columns of smoke indicated the progress of the fight. It also served to indicate the position of the rebels to the artillerists. The shelling was rapid and must have produced terrible havoc in the rebel ranks. Our men were victorious here. The rebels were repulsed, our rifle pits regained, the field covered with heaps of slain and wounded rebels whilst our loss was comparatively small. The 111 PV who fought here lost but 5 killed and 16 wounded, whilst hundreds of dead rebels lay in front of and around them.

Along the rest of the line there had apparently been but little fighting till about 1 P.M. A terrific cannonading from the rebels right and centre was then begun, such as is seldom heard even on fields of battle. A last desperate effort was made to break our left and centre. The air was alive with the shrieking missiles of death. Our men were, however, prepared for the desperate attack. Though not as much artillery in position as the rebels, though our troops were not as closely massed as theirs who came sweeping like furious waves before a tempest towards our lines; though for a time the onward sweeping tide seemed invincible; though some of our guns were silenced, and some of our positions taken, the rebels were finally driven back in confusion their columns shattered and broken, the ground covered with their wounded and dead, and many of their men prisoners making our victory the more complete. "You must do some desperate fighting to whip us, boys, for the flower of our army is here" said a rebel prisoner the day before, in my hearing. That flower withered on Friday the 3rd. The day was ours and with it the victory of the battle.

My horse had been sent back, as our hospital was again being moved, for fear it would again be exposed and for hours I searched ineffectually for them. I was faint and sick. The heat was almost insufferable. I walked till I gave out, put wet leaves in my hat and rested—walked on again, obtained some coffee and a cracker from H. Hays[8] of our regiment, started for our hospital again, which was about two miles farther back than it had been. It was in the woods, on the side of a hill, on the right bank of Rock Creek. I found Genls Hancock and Gibbons[9] there, both wounded and thousands of others men and officers of our own corps, and more were constantly being brought in. Of our regiment there were many scattered about in different hospitals and some were on the field of battle in the hands of the enemy.

Just before coming to the hospital I saw Capt J. C. Hilton near the spot where the hospital was in the morning. He was wounded in thigh, the bone being shattered up to the hip joint, and the surgeons said there was no hope of his recovery. I was informed of these facts and requested to announce them to him. He was lying on the ground, under the shade of a tree, by the side of a brook, attended to by one of his men. My task was a delicate, unpleasant and sad one. When I told him that probably his wound would be fatal, he told me he had feared it, but it seemed he never so fully realized it as then.

His eyes filled with tears, deep emotions were traced on his youthful countenance, he cast a glance upward and lay silent "Chaplain, what does it take to constitute a Christian?" He was very anxious about his soul. He had been piously trained, had been a good boy, it seems, but for some years had been rather careless. After conversing awhile on the subject of religion, he spoke about his mother and sisters. Were it not for them death would be easy. He loved them tenderly and wanted to live for their sakes. His deep feeling moved me deeply—he was overwhelmed with emotion—he, his servant, and I all of us wept. He said he did not want to be taken to the hospital— he must die anyhow and would as soon die where he was as anywhere else. "Bury me," he said as if utterly hopeless of recovery, "under this tree." His leg has since been amputated and strong hopes are entertained of his recovery.[10]

Sergt Wm Brown, Co I was among the missing. I felt very anxious on his account, for I could hear nothing of him. On the morning of July 4th I had the pleasure of finding him at our hospital, severely wounded through the thigh. He with others had been inside the rebel lines. He was cheerful, but suffered considerably. I mounted my horse and proceeded to the front of our regiment. They occupied the same position as previous day. A squad being sent to carry together the bodies of our wounded I accompanied them.

On the 2nd our regt retained the position taken in the morning till 4 1/2 P.M. They were then marched by the left flank for the distance of about 1/2 mile, where the battle was raging fearfully at the time, the enemy driving our men. Back of the house in which I found Forbes was a meadow, beyond this some woods in which our regiment was formed in line of battle and faced by the rear rank, our regt thus becoming the right of the Brigade, having been the left in the morning. They lay in the woods about 10 minutes, then advanced into a wheat field, where they relieved other troops, and commenced firing. After firing about 5 minutes the command to advance was given, immediately after which Col B[rown] was wounded, at the same time losing his sword. Capt Reynolds took command of the regt. They moved forward on the double quick, driving the rebels before them beyond a ledge of rocks, to which the regt advanced. Being in danger of being outflanked, the brigade retired, pursued by the rebels, and again occupied the position held in the morning.[11]

I passed on the 4th over the ground where the regt had fought on the 2nd. Beyond the wheatfield was a meadow, beyond that some woods. There were many rocks and bushes beyond behind which the rebels had hid. But so suddenly did our men charge on them, that they threw down their arms and surrendered. Our regt had passed over the meadow and through the edge of the woods to a brook and across this to a high ledge of rocks. Guns, bayonets, and bayonet and scabbards, cartridge boxes, and cartridges, haversacks and canteens were thrown and scattered in all directions.

Among the dead we soon recognized those of our own regiment—Talmadge Co I.[12] Cochran Co C.[13] Taylor[14] and Marsh Co B.[15] and Corbin Co D.[16] They were carried to an apple tree, under who's shadow they had fought, I offered a prayer and left the bodies there to be buried.

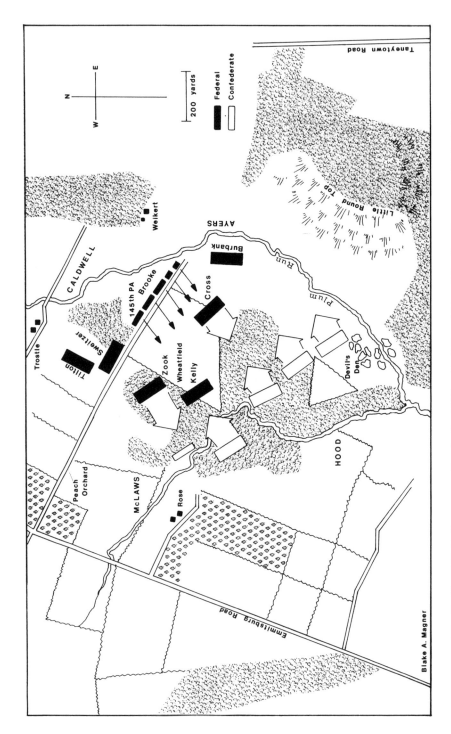

The Battle of Gettysburg — action in the "Wheatfield" and Rose Woods, afternoon of July 2, 1863.

Immediately to the right of the ledge of rocks were our sharpshooters, some of them behind trees, firing constantly. I saw the tree, behind which some were posted, a few days later, its barks cut on its sides by rebel bullets aimed at our sharpshooters. Whilst looking for our dead a bullet, perhaps aimed at some one of us whistled past us, warning us that we were exposed to rebel sharpshooters.

I was requested by the Major of 64th N.Y.[17] to hold services in his regt. I did so immediately after leaving our dead. The men were behind their breastworks, I stood in front of them. Brisk skirmishing was going on all the time, rebels and our men and rebels as well as our men could be seen running and firing. A rebel flag was also seen at the edge of the woods. Worship at such a place, at such a time, with fearful scenes just enacted and being enacted, was very solemn. I thanked God that we had been spared, prayed for the many wounded and remembered the relatives and friends of the killed. The soldiers felt deeply and many were moved to tears.

I passed on to our regt and was going to hold services there. But just then I saw a regt of our troops marching forward where the skirmishing was going on. A rebel battery concealed in the woods opened on them, enfilading the regiment. The regt faced about and retired—one shell passed over them, then came grape and canister, which struck directly in front of us. I was advised to retire. Whilst doing so a shell passed directly over my head and unpleasantly near and struck by a barn in which my horse was tied.

I returned to the 2nd corps hospital, visiting several others to look for wounded of our regt. I found Lt G. H. Finch,[18] Co E, since dead. He was wounded through l[eft] thigh and r[ight] ankle—and suffered greatly. He was faithful and brave—peace to his ashes.

In the afternoon it rained very hard. There was not a hospital tent at our hospital. Some of the wounded were in shelter tents which sheltered them poorly, others lay in the rain and mud, covered with a woolen or rubber blanket—or nothing at all. I labored to shelter them till I was wet through, and returned to my tent very weary and sick. It was a sad sight to look at the hospital at any time, but especially when those severely and mortally wounded were thus exposed. And nothing could be done for them. After the rain I with Stallman, Co I[19] got some hay and placed under the wounded. I gave my rubber blanket to one of our men, my woolen one to Wm Brown, and tore another woolen one belonging to Lt Col McCreary and divided it between E. Allen and H. Mann Co I.[20]

What a hospital on or near the field of battle is can only be known by those that have seen one. There were between 2000 and 3000 wounded in our 2nd corps hospital. In 1st Division there were two operating stands, where the Surgeons were constantly consulting about operations and were performing amputations. Heaps of amputated feet and hands, arms and legs were seen lying under the tables and by their sides. Go around among the wounded and you witness the most saddening and sickening sights. Some are writhing with pain, and deeply moaning and groaning and calling for relief which cannot be afforded them. The finest forms are horribly disfigured and mutilated.

Wounds are found in all parts of the body. Here lies one with his leg shattered, the flesh torn by a shell, nothing but shreds being left. There lies one shot through the abdomen, the intestines protruding—his life cannot be saved, perhaps even opium gives him but little temporary relief. He is but waiting to die. Here lies one with his arm almost severed from his body—waiting for amputation. There lies one young and once handsome shot through the face and head—his eyes swollen shut and covered with a yellow, putrid matter, his hair clotted with blood, his jaws torn, and a bullet hole through each cheek. Some of the wounds are dressed, some not. From some the blood still oozes, in others maggots are perhaps found. Perhaps they are poorly waited on, there not being nurses enough. No physician may have examined their wounds and dressed them. Their physical wants may not have been attended to. They long for home and their friends, but they cannot get to the one, the other cannot come to them. Through neglect, perhaps, they die. They are buried in their clothes, without shroud, without coffin, perhaps without religious services and a board to mark their resting place. The hospital soon becomes foul, especially in summer—the stench sometimes being almost intolerable. Medicines may be scarce, the food unpalatable—perhaps scarce. Near the battle field of Gettysburg many barns for miles were filled with wounded, many of whom had neither surgeons, nor nurses, nor food.

On Sunday July 5th, the enemy having retreated, our regt left the field of battle at 5 P.M. went to a place called Two Taverns where they remained till Tuesday morning the 7th. I was sick on the morning of the 5th and concluded to go somewhere in the country to rest and recuperate. I first buried E. Allen, who had died at 8 the evening previous, took the names of all our wounded and did all I could for them. I then went to Littlestown about 10 miles distant arrived there about 2 P.M. called on Rev Henry[21] of our church, who referred me to Jacob Sterner one of his members, 2 miles from town, at whose house I was kindly entertained. They are old people, plain German Pennsylvania German farmers, living well. I visited their neighbor, Mr. LeFevre, several times, whose three sons were well educated at Franklin and Mercer college,[22] and whose two daughters were quite interesting, played and sang well, and the younger of them was not only intelligent, but good looking. I enjoyed their society, and found it real and pleasant recreation. On the morning of the 7th I started back to our Hospital with Rev Henry, he having his saddle bags with bread and cakes, and I having eggs, butter and bread for our wounded. Lt Finch was dead. Black and Hilton and most of the others of our regt were doing well.

Lt Lewis[23] had his leg amputated. He looked feeble and sallow, suffered a great deal (had been lying on the field till a rebel for 25 doll[ar]s brought him into our lines to a house to their rear, but they stole his water canteen, his money ab[out] 80 dollars, haversack et cet.) and could not sleep. He has since then died. He was a noble young man, knew a good deal about military affairs and made a good officer. He was brave, ambitious and hopeful. There was an innocence and simplicity about him, which were well calculated to gain ones affection. His loss is felt severely by us all. We loved him, we admired him. He is one of the many truly noble sacrifices given to our country. He

Gettysburg

Lieutenant Horatio F. Lewis, Company D. Killed at Gettysburg.

was calm and resigned when I saw him, and frequently, I was told, was found praying. The thought of his death greatly saddens me, for I loved him and had great hopes for him. Never shall I forget how willingly he once received my reproofs for what turned out to be a sham duel.

Lt Birtcil Co F[24] was wounded in the arm, but will recover. Lt Hamlin Co I was wounded in the heel. Capt Geo Griswold Co I was wounded in the hand. It was regarded as a slight wound. He went to Philadelphia. Erysipelas set in and he has since died. He was universally beloved. There was a peculiar amiability and gentleness about him which were very winning. The news that he would probably die surprised and saddened us, and when the news came that his spirit had gone "Home," our hearts were filled with grief. Alas! that so often the bravest and dearest and best are taken from us. He was still very quite young, had the prospect of a long, useful and happy life before him. I can yet scarcely realize that he is gone. Farewell Brother, we shall meet again!

Another of our officers has died since the battle, though not from wounds—Lt Grant Co B. He was taken sick at Thoroughfare Gap with Pneumonia, was sent to Georgetown hospital, where he died. He was faithful, hopeful, ambitious, had more than a common education, and was generally well liked. He was brave and patriotic—unswerving in the performance of his duty. Through sickness he escaped the dangers of the Gettysburg battle, but his appointed hour was come, and death found him, when none of us expected it. His mind was inquisitive, and somewhat inclined to skepticism, as I found in some of our discussions in the Bible class last winter. But he was honest in his doubts and tried earnestly to discover the truth.

Lt Finch, Lt Lewis, Capt Griswold, Lt Grant—four of our youngest, bravest, best officers died in July. I trust they have gone to their reward in heaven. Lt Finch died July 6th, Capt Griswold the 16th, Lt Grant the 14th, Lt Lewis the [blank].[25] "Brothers we shall meet again."

I was desirous of remaining with our wounded; but as another battle was soon expected, and as our troops were moving, all the surgeons of our Division, except 6, and chaplains, except one, were ordered to join their regts. I bid the boys farewell and started with Rev Henry for the battle field. We rode to the left where our regt had fought and to the position occupied by the rebels. They had buried some of their dead, others had been carried together ready for burial. The stench was fearful, almost intolerable. The bodies, some horribly mangled lay their *[sic]* five days exposed to the sun—black rotting, full of worms and for days after I saw them there unburied.

Confederate dead gathered for burial at the southwestern edge of the Rose Woods.

Beyond the ledge of rocks where our regt fought were woods in which our shells had made fearful havoc, tearing the trees and limbs and scattering them in all directions. The dead there indicated that beyond that ledge of rocks, their ranks must have been thinned by our men. We rode along the field towards Gettysburg. Everywhere were seen the indications of the havoc made by rebel shells in our lines. We did not go where the rebels had fought. There were broken guns and caissons and dead horses in great abundance. On cemetery hill most of the horses of some batteries must have been killed, judging from the number lying about there.

We entered Gett[ysburg] and saw the Luth[eran] College and Seminary at a distance. I called at the house of Prof Stover,[26] but did not find him in. The city did not seem to be much injured, nor did the property seem to have been wantonly destroyed during the rebel rule. I had a passing introduction to Dr. Baugher,[27] bid farewell to Rev H[enry] and started to join the regt which had gone towards Taneytown. Near Gettysburg every road and field farm and house and barn indicated that troops had been there and that a great battle had been fought. With what feelings I left that field! We had suffered severely, but ours was the victory. It was a glorious victory. The haughty foe threatening Harrisburg, Philadelphia, Baltimore and Washington just before that, was checked, repulsed, his ranks thinned to the number of 40,000, his hopes vanquished and was pursued by a victorious, hopeful brave army.

The monument to the 145th Pa. Inf. on Brooke Avenue at Gettysburg

CHAPTER

8

RETURN TO VIRGINIA

"The Delay was to me Inexplicable."

July 7 - 28, 1863

On the evening of the 7th, after a lively ride from Gettysburg, I joined our reg[imen]t near Taneytown, soon after they arrived there. They had just received a large mail, the first since we left Fairfax Station Va three and a half weeks before that. I felt somewhat lost in the regt and somewhat homesick, for so many of my dearest and best friends in the regt were absent. The regt looked so small too, there being only about 100 men, and less than that number who carried muskets.

When we left Taneytown Wednesday morning July 8th it rained hard. Instead of abating, it increased. We were soon wet through to the skin—india rubber blankets being no complete protection against such a rain. For hours it poured down upon us, deluging us. Houses were carefully closed to keep out the beating rain, the heavens looked dark; the fields were flooded; the brooks were greatly swollen; the roads were covered with water, which in many places formed rapid streams. Through this fearful rain, which I had perhaps never before seen equalled in violence, the men had to march rapidly, seldom halting to rest. They had to wade through the deep mud and streams. Their feet became sore and some gave out, who have not yet recovered. In the afternoon the rain ceased. We struck a good pike and marched to within 4 miles of Frederick.

I bought a horse in this camp for $150 and immediately started with the mail for the city. Before reaching it my horse was very lame, having no shoes on its two hind feet. I could not have the horse shod that evening, could not find room for it in the livery stable, could not have it put in Mr. Harrison's stable, there being another horse there, and after much trouble and anxiety had it put up in Dr. Geo[rge] Diehl's stable.

I slept that night at Mr. Harrison's house. Next day I started with bread and socks and shirts for some of our officers and men to join the regt It was a warm day. We marched rapidly through a hilly country, struck Burkettsville (shook hands there with Rev Nixdorf[1]) where we halted awhile for the night, we thought. About dusk we were ordered forward—our men very tired. Lt Jewett[2] being sick was left at Burkettsville. We passed over South Mountain and camped on the side of a stony hill. We were off again early next morning July 10th. I saw Dr. Reynolds[3] of Irish Brigade, quite a literary character, who recited me one of his poems. This was another very hot day. The march was again a severe one. Firing was heard some miles in front of us. We crossed Little Antietam Creek and Antietam, passed through Kabysville,[4] and left Antietam battlefield on our left. That night we halted in a wheatfield. All the indications were that a fight would take place there, and at one time our horses were sent to the rear and a place for a hospital chosen.

Next morning Sat[urday] July 11th we had but a short march to Jones Crossing along the same road over which I passed last September from Hagerstown to Sharpsburg. Skirmishers were sent out, who were soon briskly engaged near some woods 1/4 mile from us. Several shells were sent in the woods, but no general engagement took place. That evening Lt Mitchell visited me, staid till quite late, and gave me much valuable information. I had just laid down in the evening when we were hastily ordered to fall in. We moved to the road only a few rods to our left—evidently to guard it.

It was very hot on Sunday the 12th. I had washed the only shirt I had with me on Saturday, and slept that night without a shirt. Sunday morning I spent in drying my shirt over a small fire, the perspiration rolling in streams from me. Could my Erie friends have seen me that Sunday morning—it might have given them a good idea of the shifts to which we are sometimes put. In the afternoon we moved into the woods where the skirmishing took place the day before. Just as we got there it rained hard and before I could put up my tent I was wet to the skin.

After dark we commenced throwing up breast works—a work than which the men do nothing more willingly. All next day we were engaged in completing them. Why battle was not given by Meade I could not divine. Our army, considerably reinforced since the battle, was all there. Provisions and ammunition were abundant. The men were victorious—victory gave them hope and confidence that the foe if attacked were ours. I felt a constant fear that the enemy might in someway effect an escape across the swollen waters of the Potomac. The delay was to me inexplicable and worried me.

On Tuesday morning the 14th our regiment were ordered to report to Gen Caldwell. When we came to his headquarters he was gone to the extreme front and had left no order for us. Having a horse I at once volunteered to hunt him and ask him where we were to go. I rode past the advancing troops, to our skirmishers who seemed to expect an engagement every moment, and rode some distance before I found the General, who was advancing cautiously. We soon joined the rest of our Division and marched forward towards Williamsport, skirmishing in our front leading the way. Just before reaching the rebel breastworks, a college, Episcopal I think, was seen to our right. Where we crossed them the breastworks were not very strong, a fact which made me feel all the more indignant that the enemy had not been sooner attacked.

We soon came to a muddy road over which some of their troops had been marched, the tracks indicating that many were barefooted. Prisoners were constantly being brought in, stragglers who had been left behind. We moved rapidly forward till Williamsport was within sight and already in possession of our troops. We here learned that the main body of the rebels had crossed at Falling Water, and immediately turned to the left towards Falling Water. A caisson was soon seen on the road, abandoned by the rebels. Near it we halted a few moments. Artillery and musketry was now heard immediately in front of us. Our men had come up with the rear guard of the rebels and attacked them.

Just as we started forward again Lt Mitchell of Gen Meade's staff came up. He had been sent to the front of the 6th corps to find out the position of the enemy—and had not yet found where they were, after riding about for hours. He felt very indignant that the rebels had been allowed to escape. He attributed it to damnable imbecility. He could find no words to express his disappointment and chagrin. "Chaplain" he said "I ought not to talk to you, for I have been swearing all morning." We rode together till near Falling Waters. Gen Caldwell and staff were on a high hill, to which Lt Mitchell and I were going to make observations with a field glass of the retreating rebels. When within feet of the summit of the hill and very near Gen Caldwell the repeat of a gun was heard and the next moment a shell came shrieking over our heads apparently but a few feet above us. We retired a few rods. There came another and another, but no more after that.

All the rebels had crossed safely into Va except the rear guard, which we captured. To the left of the position we occupied at this time the rebels had thrown of some breastworks on the crest of a hill, farther still to the left stood an old barn and house. The rebels were there just before we arrived. Our cavalry were about to charge on them when they made signs of surrendering, but finding out that there were not as many of our cavalry as they expected they basely fired on them killing some, wounding others, then retreating. Our dead and wounded and also those of the rebels were there when we arrived.

We were moved a few rods to the right into an apple orchard. Here we remained till next morning. No orders came of any kind, not even to pitch tents. All seemed to be greatly disappointed at Meade's failure to attack them. Our officers came together that afternoon and could not express their regret at the course that had been pursued. An attack on Monday might have shortened this war by many months. We were nearly or quite as strong as before the battle at G[ettysburg] for we had been reinforced; Lee was much weaker. We whipped Lee at G[ettysburg] how much probable that we could do so at Williamsport. The greater part of his army might have been captured. The river being so high would have prevented Lee's escape if attacked in time. If whipped again a panic would have seized his troops and thousands on thousands would have been captured and nothing but a miserable broken, scattered, hopeless, forlorn remnant would have been permitted to escape. It was believed too that the rebels were short of ammunition and supplies generally, which has since been confirmed. To expect them to attack us seemed like the sheerest folly. Four corps' Generals favored the attack, as many opposed it—Meade favored it—why then didn't he give the command: forward? As some one has said he should have done like Napoleon, given battle first and called a council of war afterwards.

I felt great respect for Meade; for he handled the troops admirably at Gettysburg and gained a brilliant victory. But now I felt that the lustre of the victory was gone. The bright sun which dawned on us at Gettysburg was as suddenly eclipsed. It was worse than Antietam. Some men make mistakes in what they do, others manifest their greatest weakness in what they failed to undertake.

Lee and his army were safely in Va and immediate pursuit was vain. For this we had been hurried from Gettysburg's bloody field—for this we had been marched through deep mud, drenching rain, intense heat to catch a few stragglers while the great body of the army was safe—could laugh at us to scorn. It makes me think of a squirrel—catch it by the tip of the tail and a few hairs remain in your hands whilst the squirrel runs briskly away, none worse for its trifling loss which it scarcely feels. All we, all the whole army had done and suffered since the G[ettysburg] battle was in vain. An opportunity was lost such as may never again be presented to us. What was to be done now? was the question. Pursue the same course taken last fall; it was the only thing left for us to do.

On the morning of the 15th we marched down the Potomac, passed over the very ground where our regt did picket duty the evening of Sept 17 last year—the day of Antietam battle. Passed through Sharpsburg, saw the place where we spent the first Sabbath in the army and held our first services, passed over the ground where our regt buried the dead and saw many other familiar places in and near Sharpsburg. At Antietam creek we struck the canal and walked along the bank between the canal and river to within 3 miles of Harper's Ferry, where we rested on the bank—a very narrow place where we could barely find room to lie down—for the night. After resting a little we bathed in the Potomac—a real luxury to persons who had been traveling in the mud and dust as long as we had.

On Thursday 16th we continued our march down the river, viewed the high abrupt hills and precipices on our right and left, with trees and shrubs and flowers and ferns and mosses covering them and hanging down the sides; saw the huge rocks so threatening in their aspect, as if ready to tumble down any moment, watched the muddy water of the Potomac, sweeping over its rough rocky beds with its "rush of mighty waters," roaring loudly like some enraged maddened monster, viewed H[arpers] Ferry, so romantically, so vividly, so beautifully, so strongly situated—so full of sad memories to us who spent our first weeks of military life there, were there initiated in its hardships and suffering, and there lost so many beloved friends. To my memory comes the name of John Fickinger, before my imagination appears his youthful, noble form; we cast a glance to the high summits of Maryland and Louden Heights. We viewed the pontoons in the middle and on the banks of the Potomac, said to have formed part of the rebel pontoon bridge destroyed by French[5] at Williamsport—why was it destroyed; marched past H[arpers] F[erry], and thanked God that we were not again required to stay at that unhealthy and unpleasant place. Saw the track destroyed across the RR bridge for fear the rebels should pursue on it our troops after evacuating the Ferry; passed beyond Sandy Hook, turned to the left, up a valley and there pitched our tents about noon. The place was, I think, called Pleasant Valley. To the east was a range of mountains, to the west Maryland Heights, on whose summit is a strong fort—commanding the surrounding country. We remained here till the morning of the 16th, busy in making out reports and payrolls. We expected to remain here for some time to rest, which we all so very much needed. But in this we were disappointed. "There is no rest for the wicked" the boys would sometimes say while marching along looking in vain for a halt.

On the 17 Sept 1862 the regt went from Hagerstown to Sharpsburg and on the 11th of July [1863] we were again on the Hagerstown road, having in the interval made a complete circuit to Falmouth and back again.

On Saturday morning July 18th we were early on the march again. We passed over the pontoon bridge to Harper's Ferry, saw the vast ruins of the arsenal and the Headquarters of John Brown glanced up the Shenandoah and on a bluff on the right about 1/2 mile distant saw our old camp. Crossed the Shenandoah into Va. How vividly I recollected the evening last fall when we were hurried down the same road. How many crossed the Shenandoah with us then who are not with us now? was a reflection that involuntarily arose. Then we had about 700 muskets, now not 100. We rejoiced when we left Va for Md and dreaded the idea of returning to the unfriendly soil of Va.

We soon passed the place where we bivouacked after that first night's march, saw the very stump where Col B[rown] had a tree cut down to make a fire and the place where Capt Walker and I crept into a corn shock to keep warm—which I however did not succeed in doing. We halted about noon near Keys Pass[6] 1/2 mile distant from our bivouac there last year. Lt Hubbard and myself got an excellent supper last fall near the Gap, about 3/4 mile from our present camp, and I invited Capt Oliver to go there with me and try to get some dinner. We thought that there could be no doubt that the pass was ours and that our pickets were there. Still Capt Oliver had his doubts and moved on more cautiously than I did, he having but lately returned from Richmond an exchanged prisoner. I rode up to the house and telling them I had been there before was at once recognized and had the promise of dinner. We took our horses into the barn yard, mine escaping and running towards the barn as I was closing the gate. When we came on the porch Capt O[live]r asked whether our pickets were at the Gap? The lady said no. We asked whether there were any rebels about? "A half an hour ago," said the lady, "two went along here with one of your men prisoners." "Chaplain let us go," said Capt O[liver] jumping up and hurrying to the barn. "Bring my horse; said I, "whilst I buy some bread." I followed the lady into the sitting room and, without my knowledge into a room where a young lady was dressing. She, however, jumped behind the door as I entered and I was too much occupied to notice her. "Bring the bread and pies to the gate," I said, thinking that if the guerrillas should come, there would be more chance of escape if on my horse. We both jumped on our horses, but were too much in a hurry to get the bread and pies. The fact was we were very near the pass and the road was such that the guerrillas might have stolen to within a few rods of us without being seen. We put the spurs to our horses and hastened back to camp, congratulating ourselves that we had safely escaped. But I was not satisfied with the result. "There is some mistake about this" thought I and concluded to go back. Capt O[liver] refused to accompany me, but Capt Lynch borrowed a revolver and agreed to go with me. Half way to the house we learned at another house that Gen Caldwell and staff had just gone to that house. Our pickets were just going out too—we had really had none there then. The report that a prisoner had been taken past there by the rebels but a short time before was confirmed. Rebels (guerrillas, I suppose) were said to hold the gap. One of the rebels who had taken the prisoner had seen a horse, which, with revolver in hand, he had said he was going to take, and was returning for that purpose. This happened about the time Capt O[liver] and I were at that house and the horse seen was no doubt mine. These facts we learned from three men, citizens between the age of 25 and 30. I verily believe that they themselves were guerrillas. Our escape had indeed been fortunate and our fears had had sufficient grounds.

I called at Mr. Conrad's where I took several meals last fall. Saw the busy negro wench and children some of which were too nearly white to belong to her husband who is about twice her age. Mrs. Conrad at once recognized me, but could sell me nothing but onions, nothing else being left. In the afternoon Col McCreary and Capt Reynolds[7] joined us. The former had been to Richmond since last with us and had been home 6 or 7 weeks. He looked well and was in fine spirits. Both were heartily welcomed back, especially by me who had been intimate with both. Both want to get out of the service, if possible, this fall. We had plenty of milk and blackberries which were much relished.

I had barely finished bathing in a creek on Sunday morning the 19th when the order came to fall in. We passed the house in which I lodged last fall, where a lady, bitter secesh, gave me her opinion about our cause. I saw her sitting on the porch busily engaged in talking to some of our officers and did not speak to her. Immediately back of the division was the provost guard with a number of deserters prisoners of whom 4 had belonged to our regt. Lt Bemis[8] among them of whom I expected much and really admired. It was sad to see him a prisoner, and the last words he said to me when he went to Washington came in my mind: "Pray for me, for I shall be subjected to great temptations."

We bivouacked in the afternoon in an open field—as we generally did. Why the woods were not chosen, but always the open field, in such heat, seemed strange. But I suppose it is damp in the woods and less healthy. As we were pitching our tent a black snake and a copperhead, with long bent teeth, were killed near us. In the evening I held services speaking of Abraham's faith—after which I took a walk with Capt Reynolds.

We marched beyond Bloomfield on Monday the 20th. By our camp was an old straw stack fit for nothing but manure, and for beds for soldiers to rest their weary limbs on.

But of course a guard must be posted over it, for fear it should be used by them. That this was looked upon as small business may well be imagined. Our weary soldiers must be taken to protect an old fast decaying straw pile belonging to some rebel; of course, the Union soldier can sleep on hard ground. Gen Hayes,[9] now commanding our corps is said to be a Virginian, this may account for it.

We remained here till the 22nd, when we were ordered forward again. I stopped at Mrs. Carter's house, where I rested a short time last fall. Mrs. C[arter] and Mrs. Tennyson were the only inmates now. A lot of darkies, however, occupied a house next to Mrs. C[arter]'s fine dwelling. Mr. Geo Carter was quite wealthy, as the fine house and farm indicates; but they are much neglected now. This time as last fall, Mrs. Carter's chickens and turkeys were not spared by our soldiers. She has two sons in the rebel army. We passed near Upperville and arrived at Ashby's Gap about dusk. Paris, a little village at the foot of the mountain, is very strong secesh. So many of the ladies there and all through Va, as far as we have gone, are in mourning, the most, no doubt, on account of friends lost in the army. Obtaining a pass from Col Brook. I went back to Paris and succeeded in purchasing some eggs (50 cts doz) milk (25 cts canteen, 3 pints) bread and butter (flour $25 per barrel).

The view from the Gap, as I saw it Friday 24th was truly grand. The sun for awhile was hid behind Bull Run mountains in the east—then gilden our mountain top and gradually sent his rays into the Shenandoah valley west of us. To the east between Bull Run and Blue Ridge mountains the valleys and mountains added variety to the scenery. The country is very broken—it is hard to tell just what it is being so varied. To the west the scene was still more grand. From the Shenandoah river heavy columns of fog were rising whilst the distant mountains were still wrapped in their mantle of mist. Soon the rays penetrated and dispelled it and before us lay the rich, fertile She[nandoah] valley, down which the shattered rebel troops were retreating. Far as the eye could reach were seen hills and valleys, woods and fields, meadows and waving grain, houses and barns and villages and through field glass, at the foot of a round mountain was seen Winchester. Grand scenes awaken grand thoughts, the thoughts of eternity, infinity, God.

I went to Paris again to get more provisions. I remained there some hours, expecting our regt to march through there, as we had already received marching orders. I learned that schools were closed and no religious services were held regularly. $15 Per quarter a scholar was the remuneration given formerly to teachers from the North. But schools and churches are scarce in Va, families living so far apart, this giving the country an air of loneliness. Miss Osborn whom I saw the evening before thought I must be a minister—judging by my voice. She was quite intelligent and not bad looking. It was 3 P.M. when we left Paris being relieved by a brigade of 12th corps, the 111th Pa regt, taking our place in the gap.

Lt Col M[cCreary], Dr. Whillden and I stopped to hear some music from a young lady who sang for me in the morning. She sang only secesh tunes as: "My Maryland" and "Virginia et cet," but we appreciated it nevertheless.

On our way to rejoin the regt we stopped to see Mr. and Mrs. Abner Furgueson, where Lt Clay and I spent a night last fall. He at once recognized me. 500 Doll[ar]s had procured him a substitute for the rebel army last January, but no more were to be had at any price. She was as beautiful as ever, She had just been asleep and was not very nicely dressed. When she came on the porch I offered her my rocking chair, but she preferred the steps, holding her baby in her lap. I cannot describe her beauty, because it is more expression than form. But all who see her acknowledge her beauty. Her language is Virginian, tinctured with the slave dialect, but that makes it all the more sweet when spoken by her.

We hastened on and soon joined the regt. Several times since we learned how guerrillas were constantly prowling around our army. Lt Col McCreary has spoken of the danger to which we had been exposed and how easy it would have been to capture us. We halted about an hour before sundown and expected to remain there that night, but in this we were disappointed. Mutton was abundant and the men supplied themselves well with it. We had just time to get supper, draw rations for the men and horses, when at dusk we marched forward again. Cannonading was heard near us and it seemed probable that we would be hurried to the scene of action to take part in the battle on the morrow.

I thought that what mortal man could do and endure in the way of marching had been done and endured by us since 14 June when we left Falmouth. I scarcely expected equal hardships, certainly none greater. But the march this evening was the severest we ever made. The men were already much fatigued by the rapid march through the heat before we started again at dusk. We were then marched rapidly forward. The road was very bad and in some places seemed impassable in the dark. In many places we could not take the road at all, it being occupied by teams, when we had to pick our way through the fields and woods as best we could. All around us in the gloom of twilight down to the darkness of midnight were the high gloomy, forest and mountains. We were going towards Manassas Gap. Up and down hill we marched, through narrow defiles, over large and small fragments of rocks, over stone wall half torn down, through muddy fields, over deep gulleys across some which the horse could scarcely jump. In crossing one of them Lt Col McC[reary]'s horse fell in the mud and threw the Lt Col to the ground, without however injuring him. We struck the RR at Markham Station. Brooks had to be waded filling the men's shoes with gravel and water and making their feet tender. We had to march along the sides of steep hills covered with loose rocks among some of which it seemed almost impossible for men and horses to get a firm footing. Then we struck the road, but it served as the bed of a stream through which the men had to wade for a long distance, it being unsafe, on account of the swampy nature of the soil, to turn from the road in the dark. Of the regt in front of us we had lost sight entirely, but a few stragglers being visible and they uncertain which way to go. I volunteered to ride forward and keep within sight of the regt in front. But I could not find it. Two of Col Brooke's aids asked me where Col B[rown] was? They had lost all traces of him. Finally Col McCreary with the few with him halted whilst I rode about to find where the front regt was. I rode in all directions, found many stragglers inquiring for Col Brooke's brigade, but no one could tell where he had bivouacked or intended to do so; got into the swamp and out again; became lost amid the ambulances and mules; went forward and backward and sideways. Everywhere heard inquiries about our brigade; went to the place where I had left Col McCreary, he was gone; went to the right found one of Brooke's aids and learned where we were to bivouac. Hunted Lt Col again, went to bivouac and found him there. It was one o'clock A.M. At three P.M. we had left Ashby's Gap and had marched very rapidly. All my bones ached. How much worse with those who had walked the whole way?

We slept in a field of oats on the side of a hill. Before us was a brook, beyond it a high mountain—a wonder they did not make us march to its top before giving us rest. The ground was very rough, but that was soon forgotten in refreshing sleep. This severe march was made by our brigade only, it having been left to guard Ashby's Gap, while the rest of the corps left that place in the morning.

Friday 25th seemed like Sunday and to this day it seems as if we spent Sunday in Man[assas] Gap. The morning was intensely hot and sultry, which together with our own weariness made us feel very uncomfortable. Some 18 or 20 of our reg[imen]t being still absent, I volunteered to hunt them and found some of them scattered all along the fields and rail road track. I had an opportunity of inspecting the road over which we had traveled.

After my night return to camp Gen Meade and Staff passed us. He wore spectacles, looked quite thoughtful, and somewhat gloomy—wearing somewhat of an unfriendly aspect. We marched back to Markham's where we had an excellent bivouac in a meadow. I am told that Meade should have said he expected the enemy to attack him at the Gap and that was the reason no battle was fought there. Perhaps another opportunity of capturing a large force of Lee's army was here lost.

On Monday (I forgot again that it was not Sunday we spent in the Gap.) On Saturday 26th we struck a familiar road and saw familiar scenes again. We passed through Rectortown, where we spent several days last fall in a snow storm and severe cold. When within sight of White Plains, where we again struck the RR, a young man stepped out of the ranks of an Ohio (66 I think) regt, 12th corps, and shook hands with me. It was a brother of Mrs. Perry Marker—whom I was glad to see.

Our camp was near White Plains. After making arrangements for supper in the village, I called at the best looking house of the place and entered into a conversation with the ladies, who were rank secessionists. Finding that they neglected to invite me to take a seat. I helped myself to one. A young lady of 20, intelligent and good looking, was not capable of casting a pleasant look at any of our soldiers. I learned from them that Mosby[10] was about, a fact which was afterwards fully confirmed. The old ladies were more communicative than the young one—they had, perhaps, no lovers in the Southern army.

The family at which Lt Col McC[reary], Capt R[eynolds] and I took supper consisted of an old man and his wife. They had a house and small garden, a few chickens and cows, and evidently had hard work to make a living with such prices as they had to pay for everything. He was willing, he said, to live under the old flag again and talked some of going North. We had some ice here, the first and last I have seen in Va. Supper consisted of ham and biscuits and milk and coffee and butter, on which we fared sumptuously. We took 3 chickens with us for which and the supper we paid 2 lbs. of coffee, which was scarce with us.

In camp we learned that some of our stragglers had a "brush" with guerrillas in which the latter were beaten. Ware,[11] one of the men waiting on the Surgeons, went a short distance from camp in the evening to get some milk and has not been heard of since. The next day Maj Bull,[12] provost Marshall of the corps, rode back with 10 or 12 men to capture some guerrillas, but he was outnumbered and his men, except his sergeant, captured, he and his sergeant saving themselves by throwing themselves from their horses and hiding in bushes whilst pursued their horses. Whether attacked by Mosby's men or guerrillas I know not. The latter are dressed like citizens, treat you kindly till they have entrapped you and rob or kill you or take you prisoner.

On Sunday the 26th we passed Tho[roughfare] Gap, halted a few minutes near an old church, in which some officers were humming a familiar church tune, passed over ground where McClellan gave us his farewell Reviews last fall on quitting the army, left our old "Camp near Warrenton" to the right, and halted in the woods for dinner. The heat was intense and some, especially of those who had been on picket all night, found it impossible to keep up.

Thoroughfare Gap, 1993.

The chicken was just done, the coffee was boiling when "fall in" was called, and Lt Col McC[reary] and Capt R[eynolds] had, to their great mortification, to leave their tempting dinner. I staid to eat mine and took my time to catch the regt. On passing through Warrenton (where we arrived last year also on Sunday) our colors were unfurled to the breeze and national airs were played, for the special benefit of the secessionists, of which this [town] is full.

After leaving W[arrenton] we took a road to the left of that taken last fall. We kept near the RR and were going in the direction of Warrenton Junction. About 2 miles from W[arrenton] I heard that our Sutler was in W[arrenton] so I went back to order him to the regt. It was a mistake, for he was not there. I learned that Meade's Headquarters were near W[arrenton] and concluded to visit Lt Mitchell. Just as I was leaving the village I saw a beautiful house and yard to the left filled with men and horses, they being Gen Pleasanton's[13] Headquarters. It was the property of "extra" Billy Smith,[14] governor elect of Va. Quarter of a mile further on elevated ground were a number of wall tents forming Meade's headquarters. After some difficulty I found Lt M[itchell] and had a pleasant interview with him. Gen M[eade] I did not see. Gen Warren[15] is a man in his prime, perhaps 35, and is highly spoken of, by the engineers at least. Lt M[itchell] accompanied me back through W[arrenton] and about 3 miles beyond.

W[arrenton] is a beautiful place, containing many fine houses and beautiful yards. The place has a clean tasty appearance. I scarcely saw a house which did not appear pleasant and comfortable. The citizens were well dressed, but complained much about high prices and general scarcity of things. I was struck with one thing, though not at all peculiar to Warrentown, at the great number of mulattos and quadroons and that so many children were whiter than their mother and their mother's husband. One day Lt Mitchell was speaking to a man well dressed and whom he took for a white, about W[arrenton] and things generally. A dark negro woman intimated to Lt M[itchell] that he was a negro, not a white man, and her husband, thereby apologizing for his lack of information. It was about dusk when I came to our bivouac about 3 miles from W[arrenton] Junction.

On Monday 21st Lt Col McC[reary], being officer of the picket, threw the line out farther, so as to include a house near our camp. There were plenty of turkeys and chickens here so Lt Col M[cCreary] asked me to go over to the house with him to see if we could get some dinner. The house, surrounded by a yard well covered with shade trees, and a farm that had been valuable, was occupied by Mr. and Mrs. Martin and their three daughters. He had three sons in the "Black Horse Company" (4th Virg[inia] cavalry)[16] who had formed Jackson's body guard.

The ladies were all in tears when we came there and looked as if they had been weeping all morning. The trouble was they had sent some of their slaves into the woods with poultry and sheep and cattle, who could not return to the house on account of the picket line, it being between them and the house. The darkies had several times approached our pickets (the Irish Brigade did picket duty that day) who threatened in words, to shoot them, when they hastily skedaddled back into the woods. By permission of the Lt Col a guard of three and myself accompanied two of the ladies beyond the picket line to let them bring in their poultry. One of the young ladies turned up her nose at the idea of having a guard accompanying them, spoke about her being glad of having brothers in the rebel service, and repeatedly sneered at the idea of guerrillas being in the neighborhood.

The old lady was as bitter as the young ones and could not hold her tongue. When the Lt Col spoke pretty severely to them, they were all in tears again and sobbed loudly. Next day when they learned that one of our soldiers had taken a sheep tears again flowed abundantly. Poor deluded people! Va, they thought, was only contending for its rights. Its sons were defending their homes and altars and firesides. We were invading hordes, come only to murder and destroy. Between the two armies they are often brought to great straits. Their farms lie neglected, their poultry, sheep and cattle and horses and grain and grass are taken from them. They receive no letters, no papers. Practically they are cut off from the rest of the world. They know little of what is transpiring around them, and much that they hear and believe is erroneous. Lee had gained a great victory in Pa—that they knew. Why he was retreating so rapidly—this they did not know. At the meals the old lady presided; the young ones generally retired to some other room—evidently to avoid us.

We lived well at their table and paid them in coffee and sugar and candles (giving them some other light besides).

Whilst near W[arrenton] Junction I went in the woods one day to read "Moore". I also examined my shirt and to my surprise found it contained some lice. Thus far I had been very successful, having found, since being in the army, only two lice, whilst the men and officers were generally abundantly supplied with them. These I found on me at this time were quite large and had evidently been transferred to me by some one else. I bathed in the evening and changed clothing, and washed my shirt next. I got rid of the lice, but how long?

CHAPTER

9

POST BATTLE STRESS

"Love for the cause did not bring these men into the service."

July 29 - September 10, 1863

Camp in the field near Bealeton Aug 7th 1863

I did not write all the preceding pages on the 29th ult., but have written a good many of them since then. I have found it no easy work to bring my journal down this far.

On 29th ult. we were very unexpectedly ordered to pack up and march. It was 4 or 5 P.M. when we started, and we marched till late in the evening, when we bivouacked in an oat field near Elktown.[1] We were up early next morning and marched several miles when we struck the road again near the place we had started from, some mistake having evidently been made. With great rapidity were we now marched through heat, halting only once before we bivouacked about noon. It did seem unreasonable to march men so rapidly, when there was evidently no necessity for it, and to halt them in the burning sun in an open field, when woods were directly in front of them. Often have I heard the soldiers say, they wished the generals would have to walk and carry a gun awhile, they would then learn to march more slowly. About noon we halted on a barren, shadeless piece of ground (once a field perhaps) covered with briers, and pitched our tents. The camp was on the brow of a hill, where the heat was most intolerable. Where we were we knew not, but supposed somewhere [between] Warrenton and Falmouth. No house, no village, no signs of industry or civilization were anywhere to be seen. I suppose we were as near being nowhere as we had ever been or well could be.

On Sunday Aug 2nd we were actually taken to the woods about an eighth of a mile distant. It must have been by some mistake or we certainly would not have been taken into the shade. There may have been some mistake in taking us there but it was done. After being cleaned the camp was an excellent one. At first the yellow jackets troubled us, but with fire and powder and by a regular seige we routed them.

We had not fared well of late, being compelled to live on "Hard tack", meat, coffee and sugar which at times seemed scarcely palatable. They may do for a march, but in camp something besides is wanted. Capt R[eynolds] paid 2 doll[ar]s for a small jar of peaches—giving an idea of sutler's prices here—and they were spoiled.

On Monday evening the announcement was made that on the morrow the paymaster would visit the regiment which was received with joy, and visions of greenbacks floated before our minds. He came on Tuesday the 4th and paid us before noon. Not having been paid since Feb 28th I recd payment for 4 months—464 doll[ar]s.

On the 4th about noon—just in the hottest part of the day—we were ordered to pack up to change camp, on account of water, it was said, which was becoming scarce. We marched but a few miles, but so intense was the heat that some dropped down and many felt sick when we halted. I was quite unwell. My head ached badly. I had, and still have, a bad cold which annoys me greatly. We are on the brow of a hill here, in an open field, covered with briars and weeds. So near each other are the different brigades and regts that very little room is given us. There are a number of fields here not one of which is under cultivation, excepting 1/2 an acre of corn and tobacco in front of our tent—the corn being already eaten by the horses and tobacco trampled under foot. The house back of us is used for Corps Headquarters. The water is not good—and some apprehension is felt for the health of the troops. At Corps Headq[uarters] there is good water—but we can get none of it.

Before me whilst writing, there is a large camp, a city of tents, beautiful when illuminated at night, containing the first and second Divisions of our troops. Beyond the gradual slope to the northwest is a valley, nearest to us a meadow, then woods apparently interminable, only a few horses being visible among the trees. Beyond this valley, in the dim, hazy distance many miles from here—north west—the Blue Ridge mountains are seen. Early in the morning they are invisible, being hid by the heavy fogs. Gradually, as the sun's rays pierce it, the mist rises from the valley and reveals the mountains nearest us, then those farther off till at last the entire ridge appears (so to the student's mind is the unfolding of truth) as if leaning against the skies, sometimes distinctly visible, at others appearing much like clouds in the horizon or like strips of high land seen from a ship on the ocean, at others wrapped in a soft mellow light giving it the appearance of clouds of mist. I like to sit and view those mountains cloud capped, hazy, sun-lit rising at such a vast distances from us elevated high above the valley, as genius above the masses and heros above cowards.

Aug 10th 1863.

On the 4th an application was sent up for a pass for me to go to Wash[ington] to express the money, but it has not come. There seems to be carelessness somewhere. Men spend their money uselessly, others loose it, some gamble it away and from others it is stolen. They are very particular at some Headquarters about the neglect and delay of those under them. Pity red tape doesn't pull both ways.

Every day the heat is intense, almost intolerable. Sometimes a slight breeze is perceptible, at others not a leaf stirs. The sky, deep azure blue, is cloudless, except along the horizon where a few white clouds appear. Throughout fly the suns rays strike with such heat, that whilst sitting in it the perspiration flows in little streams from us. Sometimes the heat makes me very sick. My head aches and feels dizzy. We have a number of cases of incipient fever in the regiment, caused no doubt by the water and heat.

Held services yesterday evening. Lt Col gave some good criticisms about the position Christ should occupy in every sermon.

I have been reading "Leisure Hours in Town," by the "Country Parson". His style is very flowing; he evidently writes without effort. But there his thoughts are so diluted that after reading awhile one longs for more solid food. To read a chapter among other things once in a while may do, but I should not like to be condemned to such reading only.[2]

How much there is around us at all times if we are only in the reflective mood. The heavens above and the earth beneath are full of suggestions. I stood in the rain the other day and looked to the east, where the heavens were bright with white and golden clouds. I looked to the west and found the heavens black with clouds, and a deep gloom hung over the landscape. How like life! To many, the only brightness of their lives is in the past, the early morning of life, whilst around them and before them all is dark. Memory has its flowers always, expectation sometimes.

Camp near Bealton August 27th 1863

I started for Washington on the 12th of August to express the money for our regt for 69th N.Y and some others in our brigade. Waited at the Christ[ian] Com[mission] rooms at Bealton about an hour and took dinner there.[3] At Warrenton Junction waited 2 or 3 hours. Stopped at the tent of Mrs. Harris,[4] whose acquaintance I made and who went as far as Alexandria on our train. Her whole heart seems to be in the noble work of relieving the wants of the sick and wounded. She assists them and herself prepares many things for them. In the heat and cold in rains and storms, at all times her labors are unremitting. She is everywhere known and highly spoken of. In the Army of the Potomac she occupies the same position that Miss Dix[5] does among the hospitals at Washington. She rode in an ambulance with the army all the way from Gettysburg. She is well acquainted with Dr. Potter and family. Dr. P[otter] told me the other day she had better go home and attend to her duties there. I admire her much.

I put up at the Washington House. On the evening of 13th I had a chill and was sick all night, lying most of the time in a semi-conscious state, half asleep, half awake, unpleasant images constantly flitting before my mind. At 2 A.M. of the 14th I was taken with Diarrhoea and vomiting, after which I felt better but still suffered severely from headache. I concluded to apply for admission to Seminary (or officers) Hospital in Georgetown and for that purpose went to the Medical Directors Office (Dr. Abbotts).

From there I was sent to Dr. Clymer's office, where Dr. DeWitt examined me and sent me back to the Med[ical] Dir[ector] with a letter for the Med Dir. I was sent to the Hospital. I presented my letter to the officer of the day (Dr. Shelton) and was assigned to ward 1, bed 12.[6] The ward contained 16 beds, 15 patients, myself included. None were too sick to be able to walk about. I was much pleased with the clean and tidy look of everything. At one end of the ward sat our female nurse (Miss Morrison) sewing. There was a look of comfort about the clean floor, the white walls and ceiling, the open windows and doors admitting air, the shutters excluding the hot sun, the white pillow cases sheets and spreads, the clean towels, the iron bedstand and mattress, the ice water in the carrier, the papers and books on the table, for which we look in vain in the army. Over my head was placed a card giving my name, rank, regt, disease and date of admission. I naturally felt a little awkward at first when ushered in the presence of so many strangers, but soon became acquainted. Miss Morrison and the two male nurses were kind and obliging, and the officers polite and sociable. I had my meals—none of the most tempting—brought to me.[7]

Among the officers was Capt Wise,[8] cavalry officer, 46 years old. His injury was contusion, his horse having fallen on him last May. He is a man of large frame, formerly weighing over 240, is genial, pleasant, sociable and kind, possessing the very qualities that win and attract. He is the most popular man in the ward and frequently attracts a circle around him. He is a man of whom much might have been made. But he is a Falstaf in more respects than size. His oaths are most shocking, his stories of the lowest kind, his language coarse and vulgar. The company around him was sometimes entertained by an account of his former vices, the most revolting and disgusting, related boastingly.

I had been there but a few minutes when Chaplains were brought,[9] my position being at the time unknown. They were universally regarded as a curse rather than a blessing. "Our Chaplain," said one "is good for nothing, except to relieve the government of money. He is too lazy to do anything and has preached only twice since he is with us. He never visits a sick man, but is always on hand when pay day comes. Damn him! I should like to see him shot. He is the only mean man we have from Ohio." Another said, "Chaplains are only fit to relieve the gov[ernment] of $116 per month," but he apologized when he found out that I was a chaplain.

One officer of cavalry afterwards related to me the following about their Chaplain. "He is a very brave and daring fellow. He was with us at one time when we were making a raid. One day whilst riding alone, some distance from the regt he saw two rebels near a spring, their horses and carbines and some mules they had captured being a short distance from them. The Chaplain secured their carbines, ordered them to surrender and brought them and their horses and mules to camp." Pretty good for the chaplain.

On the 21st, I was, at my own request discharged from the hospital. I spent the day in Washington, took dinner with Lt Col McCreary on his way home on sick leave, with quartermaster Payne and Dr. Steward of Alexandria, at the Metropolitan. I purchased a number of articles for the regt, staid till pretty late in the evening and returned to the hospital about 11 P.M. Left on the morning of the 22nd for the regt.

The cars were a short distance from Alexandria where they stopped. Another train coming behind us whistled when a few rods from us. I saw the train coming and knew they were stopping, hence was not surprised. But not so with the other passengers in our crowded car. They thought the train was rushing at great speed into ours, expected a great crashing and smashing of cars. They jumped up, thronged the narrow passage, rushed for the doors, pushing and squeezing each other in the hurry and confusion. Some in their hurry tried to get out of the small windows. One stuck when half way through, another succeeded in reaching the ground, somewhere on the side of a steep embankment. How he got out or lit, he did not know, but found a lump on his head, which indicated that he had struck it. Altogether the scene was very ridiculous, and when the consternation had subsided we all had a good laugh over it.

Camp near Bealeton, Aug 28th 1863

For the first time in my life I this afternoon witnessed an execution the shooting of two deserters.[10] (One was shot last Friday;[11] but I did not see it.) They belonged to the 2nd Div of our Corps. At 3 P.M. the troops of that Div were drawn up to form three sides of a square. The guns and swords were glistening in the bright sun, the flags were floating on the breeze, officers were riding about proudly on the steeds as if on parade and the whole formed an imposing scene. Among the soldiers there was considerable feeling, but some could not refrain from rude jokes and profanity. "Quite a healthy place this" said one, "where you've got to shoot men to start a graveyard."

When the troops were all there a mournful tune was played by a brass band, marching with slow tread towards the scene of execution. Then came 15 or 20 soldiers with guns loaded, who were to shoot the prisoners. Then came 16 men carrying on their shoulders 2 black walnut coffins. They were followed by a chaplain having one prisoner on each arm, and a Bible in his hands. One of the prisoners was about 20 years old and looked very pale; the other was over 30 and looked more calm and composed. Then came some 20 guards with bayonets fixed.

A deep solemnity was everywhere manifest as their procession marched with slow and solemn tread towards two graves—the place of execution. The band halted near the graves and ceased playing. Those that were to shoot the prisoners.[12] The coffins were placed on the ground one beside each grave. The prisoners advanced and stood in front of the coffins facing the troops. Orders were read to all the troops. The Chaplain then made a short prayer and bid them farewell. An officer stepped up and bandaged their eyes. They pulled off their coats and carefully folded them, the one throwing his by his side, the other laying his on the coffin. The officer after bandaging their eyes, told them to kneel on their right knee and shook hands with them. The older one then immediately stretched out both hands, as if to say, I am ready. The officer then gave the command—Take aim!—Fire!—Both fell instantly, the one forward, the other on his side. They uttered no groan, scarcely moved. Not being quite dead each was shot again by a soldier stepping close to them. Their bloody bodies were placed in the coffins, after the troops had been marched by them, and were buried. I turned away—sick and sad but felt that the execution for desertion was just. Two women were present—the rest were nearly all soldiers.

Camp near Bealton, Va Aug 31st 1863

Last Saturday 29th I attended a Chaplains' Convention in the chapel tent of the Chr[istian] Com[mission] at Bealton. There were some 28 or 30 chaplains present. The discussion turned chiefly on the lack of transportation and respect for chaplains and the law that when not on duty they were to receive no pay. I expressed my regret at this, wished that some other subject had been discussed, thought chaplains themselves were to blame, and that judgement must commence with ourselves. During the discussion the news was received that Sumpter and Wagner were ours.[13] The news was received with much applause. A verse of the Hymn—"My country tis of thee" was sung and a prayer of thanksgiving offered. I was the youngest man there, most of them were middle aged and some grey headed.

Lt Mitchell of Gen Meade's staff was with me from the eve of 28th till morn of 29th and we had a good time, conversing about past, present and future.

I called on Col Brooke yesterday to see about my resignation. He said: That if I were like some chaplains I would have no difficulty in getting out of the service—that he would give them each an endorsement as would secure that end, because their services could well be spared to the country. Of 2 or 3 chaplains he spoke rather severely—had no respect for them—seemed loth to have me go. But after urging the matter and stating my reasons, he said perhaps I might by explaining the matter in my resignation, have it accepted.

We were just at supper when we saw a lot of conscripts and substitutes for our regt march in camp in charge of Capt Stiles. There were 169—two having escaped at Philadelphia—and they were nearly all substitutes. They are a motley looking crowd—Germans, Irish, Americans, some very ignorant and scarcely speaking the English language, others quite sharp and intelligent. They had been very badly treated on the boat from Phil[adelphia] to Alexandria—worse than slaves in a slaver they declared. For whiskey some paid a dollar a drink or from 30 to 40 doll[ar]s per canteen—3 pints. Bread 50 cts small loaf. The place in which they were crowded was filthy. They were not allowed to go on deck. They were ravenously hungry when they got here, but were in good spirits and looked like a jolly set.

Their remarks were amusing. "Get me some whiskey," was the first thing I heard when they were halted in front of headquarters. Some were too ignorant or unwilling to answer to their names. "Any pies or turkey," said one—as if such things were to be had here. "I wish the man was here for whom I'm here," said a substitute. "I wish I was with the old woman tonight," said an Irishman rather gloomily, but with much earnestness, as if he really meant it. "I wish I was on a ship the wind blowing so hard that it would take ten men to hold the Captain's hair on," said one fellow who looked as if he had been a sailor. There was one tall, lean, gaunt looking fellow six feet five inches high. "Is it cold up where you are," said a small fellow by his side looking up at him.

They were in good humor after their supper of crackers, which some declared they could not bite, of salt pork, which they complained of because not cooked for them and coffee. "I have eaten so much pork," said one, "that I am ashamed to look a hog in the face." A number asked how far it was to the Rappahannock and whether we have any troops on the other side of the river etc. as if meditating on desertion in that direction. We keep them under strong guard now. One tried to desert on the boat and managed to obtain citizens clothes. There is a prissy, sharp looking fellow, in the corner of whose eye desertion lurks.

They have plenty of money, and many seem to place but little value on it. Some staked 100 dollars a time on their way down here. One said he had lost over $10,000 in his life by gambling, another that he had lost more than he ever expected to be worth again. Scarcely had they got to their camping ground when I saw some squatting on the ground and playing cards by moonlight. When I went there this morning I again found small parties engaged in playing cards. There are no doubt well trained thieves and pick pockets among them. The tall fellow had his watch, valued at $90, stolen last night besides some money. Another gave me his watch last evening for fear it would be stolen. Some were without blouses and blankets, these things having been stolen from them before they left Phila. They are very profane, much more so than our men. One old German seems to take special delight in counting his money and refused to send it off. They are now being searched for the purpose of finding the watch and 125 doll[ar]s stolen last night.

One man had a bad fit. How the Doctors came to pass him I know not, he having been sick for some months. Looking on the tent on which he was lying and scratching it, he cried out most piteously "what is that after me, what is that after me." Saltz[14] set him all right again. I found a party gambling but soon stopped it.

Sept 2, 1863

Four substitutes have already deserted since their arrival here, and we have no trace of them yet. But it is said they cannot get through the picket line. If caught they may be shot. One loses all sympathy for the deserters that are shot, when their character is taken into account and the fact that many come with the full intention of deserting, knowing at the same time the penalty inflicted for it.

Night before last I found some men gambling and made them stop it. But scarcely had I turned around when they were at it again and continued at it till 3 o'clock the next morning. Some gambled last night till 2 this morning. Money seems to be of little value in their eyes. How to stop this vice I do not know. I have thought much on the subject, have spoken about it to the men and officers, but I have found no practical way of checking it. I fear that neither persuasion nor threats, neither entreaty, nor punishment will stop it.

I heard one of the substitutes singing finely last evening. He is a Mexican, was wounded and captured lately at Puebla, and is much concerned for the fate of his country. He claims to have been a Captain of engineers, and a brother of the Mexican Minister of war, and seems to be well acquainted with the topography of Mexico. A few words from me favorable to Mexico and against the French invasion at once seemed to gain his favor and admiration. He insisted on presenting me with a fine gilt-edged Bible, which I [saw] was the gift of his wife; and asked me to give him another Bible as a keepsake. I of course refused the gift, but he forced it on me. What to make of him I do not know. Time will undoubtedly develop his real character.[15]

We have some Frenchmen among the substitutes, who have lately landed in this country and scarcely speak English. One of them is an enthusiastic admirer of Napol[eon] 3rd and says he does not know whether the North or South is right and would as soon fight for one as the other, but that fate brought him into our army and therefore he will fight for our cause. That love for the cause did not bring these men into the service is very evident from the remarks and fact that they did not come as volunteers but as substitutes.

A German from Hanover, two weeks in this country came to me this morning to ask me to assist him to get out of the service, which I politely refused to do. His wife and children (4) are still in Germany. A friend of his, a weaver, cheated him into the army, he says. He got only $150, "his friend" pocketing the rest. The little finger of the right hand is off, which the examining surgeon did not see. He is dreadfully afraid of a battle, speaks gloomily of the condition of his family, if he should be killed and would willingly give up the money he received as substitute. Poor ignorant simple-minded fellow, he does not yet know that getting into the army binds a man like a marriage contract. Another German, 58 years old, awkward and toothless, had been told he would do some work here and that he would not be compelled to carry a musket, for which, he says, he did not come down here. He tried hard to get my influence to accomplish this end, and intimated that he had plenty of money, and would not leave my labors unrewarded. I, of course, refused to intercede in his behalf.[16] Another had been in the cavalry service and wants to enter it again, which can perhaps be done.

At 1 o'clock this morning the camp was all astir, horsemen were riding about, men were gathered in groups talking with each other and much anxiety was manifested on the part of some. A report had come that the rebels were across the river and preparing to make a dash into our camp. This would have been a most opportune time for them, the troops of our corps being out on a reconnaissance, and nothing but the sick and bummers and substitutes and guards being left behind. We were ready for the attack that was not made. There being no firing nor warlike demonstrations of any other kind, we retired and slept undisturbed till morning.

6 P.M. [September 2]

A German subst[itute] of Co K has just been here, pale and trembling with excitement because he heard some say near his tent that they were going to butcher him, because he deserted 2 years ago from a regt near Phil[adelphia]. Poor fellow, he believed they were going to kill him tonight. He is not altogether right, but is evidently partially insane as his tent-mate intimated to me. I have again been solicited by a German to have him freed from carrying a musket—he wants to be a teamster. These requests are becoming quite annoying, being so frequent and of such a character that I cannot possibly comply with them. There are some here, as in every regt, who would willingly do anything to get rid of carrying a musket and entering a battle. An old German (58) just now told me how difficult for him to drill. "An old dog never learns to dance and so geht es mir"[17] he said. "Could I not become a cook?" said the 43 old German this evening. "I was Sergt Major 3 years in the West Indies, can't you use your influence to have me made corporal here?" said a Dutchman. To me they bring their complaints and unburden their souls, and my influence they seek when they want to effect any changes, as if that were all powerful. A most unenviable position is mine. I do not like to refuse my aid and yet cannot give it when so unreasonably requested.

9 P.M. [September 2]

Whilst walking with Maj R[eynolds] this evening in the beautiful starlight towards a band discoursing sweet music, we were arrested by other music in the woods near us. A number of our men had left the noisy camp and gone to the woods, where alone and uninterrupted they held a social prayer meeting. There is something so solemn in those meetings, such a depth, so much feeling and serenity. The solitude and quietness of the place, the dense forest around you, the silence unbroken except by your own voice and its echo, the evening hours with its darkness through which the trees and a few stars look upon you as if the eye of God, are well calculated induce a devotional state and draw the heart to God. It makes me think of the first time I entered a forest to pray, with one of my classmates at college. How fervent that prayer. It seemed like direct communion with God. And as we arose the tears were streaming down my eyes. These meetings show too that rel[igion] has not died out in our regt.

Friday Sep 4th 1863

A subst[itute] of Co D has just unburdened his heart to me. His is really a pitiable case. He declares he has served 11 years (and is not 25 years old) in the navy from which he claims to be a deserter, was also in the Confederate Army, has C.S.A. pricked on his arm and a secesh flag. On board a ship where he gets no grog he gets along finely, he says "but on land I am always crazy, I cannot let drink alone." He was drunk, he says, when he enlisted and wants to return to the navy from which he deserted—wanted me to write to Sec[retary] Welles,[18] who must know him as he has a list of those serving in the navy. "The difficulty is I am constantly getting another name," he said. But why do you change your name? "Oh, I don't know" he replied smiling. He claims to have lost 400 lately—that amount having been stolen from him. "I should have had it again had I been free last night," meaning no doubt that he would have taken that amount from the man he suspected of being the thief or from some one else. The fact is however he was not free last night, but walked up and down a beat beside a guard, with his hands tied behind him, a punishment for disobeying orders. He is a drunkard, a pickpocket, a liar, and everything else that's bad, I suppose; is already tired of the service and wants to get out of it. Unless he reforms he is a ruined man. "I am not 25," he said "yet my hair is gray"—taking off his hat. "Drink, drink has done it." Another noble nature destroyed—ruined perhaps irretrievably. It saddens one to see such a one, and reflect on what he might be, and on your own inability to change him.

By constant and severe application you may acquire learning and reputation; hard work changes a wilderness into fruitful fields and populous cities and deserts into gardens; labor and skill transform the rough marble into beautiful statues; but often all our labor and skill and prayer are in vain in our attempts to change the mind from error to truth and the heart from sin to holiness. The noblest work is also the most difficult, and most frequently fails to accomplish its ends. All other objects on which you work are under your control—your power to shape them is greater than their power of resistance, but the will of another is a power you cannot force—its resistance is invincible.

We are again feeling the monotony and tediousness of camp life. After being in camp as long as we have a change is anxiously looked for. To some even a battle is welcome on ac[coun]t of the change and excitement it affords. One grows so tired of hearing and obeying the same commands and doing the same thing, hearing the same sounds and seeing the same forest and deserted houses and desolated farms every day. No strange face is seen—scarcely ever a citizen, a lady perhaps not for weeks or months and nothing but soldiers, all dressed alike and engaged in the same duties. It is so different on the march where constant changes occur. If the scenes of nature were grand here it would not be so dull. But where the fields are deprived of fences, utterly neglected, covered with briars and weeds or else used as camps, or for roads there is but little to excite the imagination or please the taste. The roads and the dust from them covering the grass and weeds and trees—everything in short—give the country a dreary, desert look. You look in vain for farming implements and the signs of industry and prosperity. The ringing laugh of children around schoolhouses is never heard. Even the barking of dogs, the crowing of cocks, the bleating of sheep and lowing of [cattle] are seldom heard. The voice of no animal save the neighing of horses, and the braying of mules, the frogs in the swamps at night, and at long intervals the notes of some lonely birds. Even the birds except crows and hawks and buzzards seem to forsake the region occupied by an army as too uncongenial for them. You see no flowers and no fields of fruitful grain and gather no fruits. The fresh youthful nature tires of these scenes and long for some corresponding more with itself.

After a dull monotonous day spent in camp I have found an evening walk taken regularly with Maj Reynolds very pleasant. The rumbling of wagons has then ceased and also the tramp of horses. The darkness hides the dreary aspect of nature, and the stars looking calmly down from heaven make the darkness welcome. They speak of calmness and peace amid the tumult of war and hope in the darkest night. For miles around us lighted tents were seen and candles and fires—those near us bright, those distant dim—looking like a vast city beautifully illuminated. Call it sentimental or what you will one has then feelings deeper and more tender than at other times. The silence and darkness render the two most active of the senses inactive; and the inward eye is opened and the whispers of the spirit become audible. Forms of other days—now gone and lost—flit before the mind, dim or distinct, as near or far in the past. Old associations are awakened and days of auld lang syne. Dreams of youth are dreamed over again. Once more we live in childhood's shining banks and enjoy pure water near the fountain of life's stream. We are home again—home is so far away to which we can not now or may never return.

Whilst walking on in night and silence and meditation we sometimes hear the rich stirring music of a brass band, loud and clear, trembling over the valleys and echoed by the mountains. We stopped, we listened, but spoke not a word. But heart and feeling were all the more active. There is something very stirring too in a drum and fife, but one tires of hearing the same calls repeated daily—at Reveille and tattoo and taps—call for drill and guard marching. But in the brass band you have a variety of tunes, the old and familiar patriotic and sentimental and the new and beautiful ones. The rich mellow tunes floating on the air thrill the heart and awaken thoughts. "How Beautiful" we often exclaimed, when language could not express the emotions awakened—which were themselves perhaps indefinite. The 2nd of July, just before we entered the field of battle at Gett[ysburg] a band struck up near us, as if to prepare us for the terrible ordeal though which we were to pass. "Never did music affect me more than that," said an officer to me the other day; and surely "Hail Columbia" and the "Star Spangled Banner" were never more opportunely played.

Ten deserters were reported this morning and four more this evening. Some of the substitutes no doubt think the death penalty will not be enforced. Efforts have been made to stop gambling, but without effect.

Sept 6th 1863

I attended another meeting of chaplains yesterday at Bealton. There was little spirituality manifested, the discussion again turning chiefly on "grievances." I am tired of such meetings of chaplains, and wish they would discuss subjects that would benefit us spiritually and prepare us the better for our work or else give up the meetings altogether. Gen Howard was severely censured for remarking in Wash[ington] Feb 22 that the chaplaincy was a failure. Though I know Gen H[oward] did not mean to say that chaplains were a failure.

Last night was the noisiest since the arrival of the substitutes, a number of whom were drunk and quarrelling. I was awakened by their loud boisterous, vulgar and profane language. Some seemed willing to fight any and everybody. Five or six walked beats along with the guard a good part of the night for gambling, drunkenness, sleeping on post and disobeying orders. A party who had been gambling last night commenced a quarrel, in which one drew a revolver and had it cocked, when it was taken from him. One drunken fellow was tied to a tree, who attracted a large crowd around him by his noise.

There was another scene in another part of the camp about 9 or 10 o'clock. A man who had been sick for several days was having a series of very violent fits. It took several men to hold him. He clenched his fist till it was almost impossible to open them. His eyes were fixed—stared. He breathed violently and with great difficulty, the white foam spirting and flowing from his mouth. He would come to, look around him, say a few words—then, as if frightened by some object at which he stared steadily, he would draw back, attempt to flee from the object, would hold out his hands as if to ward it off, would utter a cry of horror which pierced our hearts and moved us with pity. I bathed his head, gave him morphine powders and applied plasters to his temples after which he found relief. He had no recollection this morning of his fits and said he had not suffered any pain.

One of the substitutes, partly intoxicated, was very profane while near me yesterday morning. I reproved him mildly when he declared he never swore, but knew plenty that did, that he utterly detested the vice. He had the impudence to tell me he was always faithful in the discharge of his duties, (which I know to be a lie), and that he would like to become an ambulance driver, not being able to march, because not fully recovered from a wound received at Fredericksburg—he being a discharged soldier. Then he had no business to come in as a substitute. Another Irish sub[stitute] stopped me this morning and informed me that though he did not belong to my church, he knew I would do him, a favor if I could. "I was a schoolmaster, am well educated and write a good hand, and should like to get a position somewhere as a clerk." He then offered to pay me, if I did so, which I politely refused—telling him to do his duty and apply to his officer for such a position. I never saw men more complaisant and more full of promises than these men and when they ask a favor, yet they are often the worst of worst of characters. My sermon the other night, in which I said some very plain and pointed things, did not offend, but has done good. During the few days the subs[titutes] have been with us they have learned to respect me. Stopping to speak to them when passing through the streets, especially when they are sick, always treating them kindly and doing little favors for them together with the report given of my character and labors by our men have made me popular among them, too much so, for they are constantly asking me to do for them, what I cannot do conscientiously. I distributed papers and books among them, all of which were gladly received. Testaments were much in demand, and a number of Roman Catholics received them eagerly, some coming to me asking for them.

A gun just now broke the quite of the Sabbath day, fired it seems near in the direction of Falmouth. The day is quiet hot, the hottest for a week or so.

Sept 7th

One of the "subs" shot off his little toe last night no doubt hoping thus to be discharged. What will be done with him I know not. A few guns in the direction of Warrenton were heard this morning. A cavalry raid into Pa seems to be apprehended. Services yesterday well attended and the effect good.

A "sub" has just been here and gave me his money, for fear it should be stolen. He is an American, has been on the coast of Africa—on a slaver—taking slaves to Cuba. Thinks it was good business because it paid him $ 75 a month. There are also among the subs[titutes] Germans, Irish, and Englishmen, Frenchmen, a Russian, a Hungarian, Dutchman, Mexican and a number who were rebels once.

Sept 8th

Already twenty "subs" have deserted. Two drunken subs are in the guard house now. Over hundred doll[ar]s were stolen last night. One man threatens to leave soon and promises his friends that when he gets home he will have good clothes and plenty of money already having time, no doubt and still expecting to do well at stealing. There has been gambling and stealing and drunkenness in the regt for the last eight days, [more] I believe, than for the whole year we were out before. It does not seem like the same regt; it being completely changed by the subs[titutes] or conscripts (or convicts as some call them) for the worse. Our guard house use to be vacant—now it is full, men were seldom tied—now it is a common occurrence; a wooden "horse" for delinquents to ride was unknown in the regt till the present—now it stands near headquarters, "a disgrace to the regt" as someone said. Our old men are heartily ashamed of the godless subs[titutes] who have so materially lowered the moral of the regt. But some of these subs are having a hard time of it, and deserve commiseration rather than blame. One had just been to see me—a Hungarian who speaks no English, but "Deutsch, Ungarinsh, Wallachisih, Zerbish and his using Turkisch." "Languages I cannot use here" he said. Some have been accustomed to high life and good society and find this life very unpleasant, nor is it made more pleasant by constant complaining. The big six foot five is still here doing well. He is commonly called the "infant".[19]

I have just witnessed a very amusing kind of fun. As many men as can get hold of it take a blanket in which a man is placed. The blanket is then successively stretched out. The man each time being tossed in the air, sometimes 15 feet or more. Not being able to control his movements in the air, he comes down in the blanket in every possible way, sometimes all doubled up, at others straight with hands and feet stretched out in a sprawling fashion; sometimes he lights on his feet, sometimes on his hand, head, side, face, or back. A drunken fellow was thrown into the blanket and tossed up. He cut the most ludicrous figure imaginable, no caricature could do it justice. He sprawled and kicked, and fell every way. His eyes stared as if intently fixed on some object. "Hurrah for the Union", he cried at one time as he went up, looking very wild, and much like a monstrous frog, of some very remote geological period. He took it all in good part, though at first made more dizzy by it. "That's right," "go it boys," "shake the whiskey out of him," the bystanders convulsed with laughter cried. Such recreations are good for the boys.

Sept 9th 1863

A post mortem Examination of the body of Baker Co A, who died very suddenly about 2 P.M., has just been held.[20] The course of his death was not discovered. His heart and brain and lungs and liver were in good condition his brain very solid and healthy. On his stomach some Jamaican Ginger was found. He had been drinking on the boat on his way down here but had not been drunk in camp. A few days ago he was relieved from guard on account of sickness. He vomited and said some one had given him something which made him sick—had drugged him. It seems that no one knows anything about him—whether he has a family or where he is from.

The two drunken fellows who were tied all day before yesterday are tied again. Three men were riding the wooden horse this morning. They seemed to enjoy it at first and made fun if it, but soon got over that.

Sept 10th

Our "subs" sometimes say and do things which are very ridiculous. One, an Irishman, on guard the other day halted Capt Lynch in the following manner; "Who the Devil comes there?"

"A friend."

"A friend! Tut, go to bed, I know no friends here."

When the vote for the governorship of Pa was taken yesterday, an Irishman was asked whether he would vote for Curtin?

"I vote for Curtin?" he said in astonishment. "I'm a Dimocrat and vote none of yer Republican tickets. Hurrah for Jackson! I'll vote for Woodward." The vote of the regt was as follows: All the officers—15—for Curtin. Enlisted men for Curtin 171, for Woodward 4.[21]

Note: The following entry, while not part of the Diary, concludes the military service of Chaplain Stuckenberg.

Camp 145th Regt Pa Vols Sep 28th 1863

Adjutant:
Sir:
I would respectfully offer my resignation for the following reasons:
My charge in Erie, having been without the services of a Pastor for more than a year,

is much in need of my presence and anxiously awaits my return. Our regiment is so much reduced in number that a larger field of usefulness is presented in my charge in Erie.

Besides myself, there are two other Chaplains in this Brigade which is smaller than a full regiment.

Hoping that you will grant my request, which is made from a sense of duty, I remain

                Your obdt Servant
                J. H. W. Stuckenberg
                Chaplain 145th Regt Pa Vols[22]

Chaplain John Stuckenberg.
Photo taken in Harrisburg, possibly in September, 1862.

APPENDIX

1

From *The Lutheran Observer* of March 6, 1863

Army Correspondence
For the Lutheran Observer.
The Effect of a Battle on a Man's
Religious Views and Feelings.

Just before entering the field of battle, the conscience of a man, not altogether dead to religion, is unusually active. He will ask himself how his account stands with his Maker, in whose presence he may soon be called to appear. The past will roll its burden of sin upon him, and hang heavily on his soul. His besetting sin will stand between him and his God to disturb his peace. Then, if ever, there will be keen anguish of soul, deep regrets and an earnest desire for purity of heart. Cards are torn from the pocket, and scattered to the winds; new resolutions are formed; a silent, fervent prayer is offered to God; passages of Scripture, thoughts of home and friends, the counsel and prayers of pious parents rush upon the mind, whilst hope and fear content for the victory and the probabilities of life and death in the other world are weighed. Never does the christian feel the real, living presence of God and his saviour, more deeply, than in such an hour; and in the thought that God reigns and watches over him, is his only hope and consolation.

Then it is, too, that the wicked manifest their utter recklessness and godlessness. The awful scene around them, stir the deep of their souls, but only to cast up mire and dirt. There are sounds in battle more fearful than the shrieking of shells, the whistling of bullets, the rattling of musketry, the thunder of cannon, the unavailing cries for help, and the groups of the wounded and dying; they are the horrid oaths uttered there by the wounded and dying, sometimes polluting the lips with the last breath with which the soul passes from the body to the judgment seat of Him whose name he profaned. I have just passed the grave of such a one. He was a youth of eighteen, kind, and brave, and patriotic, but very profane and irreligious. He entered the battle of Fredericksburg, ridiculing those that attempted to dodge the shells, and cursing and swearing. He was wounded in the engagement and borne from the field, but only to die.

Danger tests the christian's faith and the skeptic's doubts. The former may find his faith give way when most needed, whilst the latter may have his spiritual eyes, which were blind before, opened in a battle. In a great crisis, in times of deep feelings, in danger, and in death, the skeptic may, as if by inspiration, have such a revelation of his own condition and his relation to his Maker, as to dispel his doubts, and create a new faith.—The voice of God, speaking so loudly there, must be heard by the soul far more susceptible of deep impressions, than at other times. Shortly before the battle of Fredericksburg, an officer in our regiment said to me, "Chaplain, I don't believe the Bible is inspired, nor that Jesus Christ was more than human, and do not think that God has anything to do with the government of this world." He was in fact a Deist, denying the overruling providence of God. During the battle of Fredericksburg, our regiment was in the very hottest part of the field, and in a few hours lost two hundred and fifteen men, out of four hundred and seventy-five. Soon after the battle I met this officer, and asked him how he escaped unhurt? He replied in a very earnest manner, "nothing but the kind Providence of God would have led me safely through such a fire." A few days ago I spoke to another officer on the subject of religion. He said, "Formerly, I was very profane, but since I am in the army I have tried to quit swearing. I also thought that God had little or nothing to do with the government of the world; but I have changed my opinion since the battle of Fredericksburg. I now believe in an overruling Providence, for otherwise I do not see how any could have escaped from such a field." To show how wonderfully some were protected, he said: "I saw there what I would not have believed, had another told me. A shell falling in a regiment just entered the field, exploded and knocked down six men. I thought, of course, that all were killed or wounded, but five of them jumped up unhurt, and hurried on the field; whilst the sixth was wounded in the leg, and his clothes were on fire, but he was still able to get to some water near by, and put out the fire."

In looking at the soldiers just coming from the field of battle, I have always been struck with the deep solemnity written on their countenances. There is no jesting, no laughing, no trifling as they look through the thinned ranks to see who are safe, and who among the killed, the wounded and the missing. You at once see, that the terrible scenes they have witnessed, did not leave them unmoved. They have shed blood and have seen it flow in streams from the wounds of many a comrade; they have been on the field of carnage, and have been at the very jaws of death, and still have escaped unhurt—and a feeling of gratitude arises in their bosoms. What they have seen and heard is indescribable, but it haunts them till the day of their death—and they are changed beings, and can never again be what they were. Thought has been busy, hurried, distracted and anxious; feeling has been excited, deep, and intense, and painful; and an impression has been made that can never be effaced, and which must either lead a man nearer to God, or petrify his heart.

J.H.W.S.
Chaplain 145th Penn'a. Vol.
Camp near Falmouth, Va., Feb. 9, 1863

APPENDIX 2

**Prayer for
A day of national humiliation, fasting, and prayer
April 30, 1863**

Lord Jehovah, Father of all! Thou first and best of Beings! Praise and glory be unto thee, that thou hast made us capable of seeking, loving and serving Thee.

Glory be unto Thee, that Thou has invited us to call upon Thee in every time and need and supplicate Thy help and direction in all our undertakings and Thy deliverance in all our dangers.

We adore, O Thou King of Kings, Thine unspeakable goodness towards this land and country. Conscious of our own unworthiness and relying on the merits of Thine every blessed Son, we humble ourselves before Thee; fearing yet loving; trembling, yet adoring.

We confess, O Lord! Thou hast done wonderful things for us and for our Fathers, Thou hast given us a goodly heritage, Thou hast often supported us signally in the days of our danger. But alas! our ingratitude has increased in proportion to Thy blessings and all sorts of transgressions have spread themselves wider and wider among us.

Thou hast visited us with dire calamities and the consequences of our sins. We have not learned Righteousness, Our unworthiness might justly provoke Thee to remove from us our inestimable blessings both civil and religious.

Yet, tho, we have sinned against heaven and before Thee, will still trust in Thy mercy. Thine ear is not heavy that it cannot hear, nor Thy hand shortened, that it cannot save; there is sufficiency in the blood of the Redeemer! Suffer us therefore Merciful Father in this day of our visitation to throw ourselves upon the merits of the ever blessed Jesus: humbled under Thy chastisement, confessing and bewailing our past offences, both national and personal and beseeching Thee to revive among us a Spirit of piety, integrity and virtue.

Above all and as the foundation of all, inspire us with a hearty reverence of Thy glorious Majesty. Give us an unwavering fidelity and earnest loyalty to the constitutional authority or our land; a prevailing love and veneration for the laws of our country civil and religious and when called to appear in defence of them, may we betray no unmanly fears, but act the part of Americans and of freemen, devoted either to death or victory and scorning a life purchased at the expense of fidelity and our national blessings.

Bless the rightful ruler of our land, the President, Bless his cabinet and all his alliances: surround him with counsellors of a true, uncorrupted American spirit, men sagacious to discover, and steadfast to pursue their country's good. Guard him from all conspiracies against his person and government. May his administration be just and wise steady in the cause of Liberty and firm in promoting the public welfare of all the inhabitants of the hostile sections of our country. For this end O God, give success to every just arrangement on sea and land. Give courage, honor and integrity to our commanders and "Those who turn the battle from our gates."

Sustain the soldier in his exposure and privations and cause him to remember Thee and put his trust in the Lord of hosts. Comfort and keep the friends whom he leaves behind and stay their hearts. Bless all those who have gone and still go forth in the defence of our flag and in the name of our government to preserve among us and to spread abroad to the remotest parts of the Earth the precious blessings of liberty and undefiled Religion.

O thou, that stillest the storm of the ocean and quellest the tumults of the people, speak peace to the rage of the hostile brethren of our land and bring this war to a safe and speedy issue. May we soon be delivered from our fears and peace prosperity and harmony be restored in all our borders.

May Thou who have gone forth and still go forth from their homes and their firesides in their country's cause be returned safe to our friendship, bringing the emblems of peace and love. That they and we may afterwards serve and adore Thee in common without fear in holiness and righteousness before Thee all in the remainders of our days.

Hear us; O Heavenly Father, Gracious God, for they Son Jesus Christ sake, to whom with Thee and the Holy Ghost, one God, be the Kingdom and the power and the glory world without end, Amen.[1]

NOTES

INTRODUCTION

1. John O. Evjen, *The Life of J.H.W. Stuckenberg*, (Minneapolis, Lutheran Free Church Publishing Company, 1938).
2. Over 500 according to Richard A. Hoehn in *Now We See Through A Glass Darkly—But We See: The Papers of J. H. W. and Mary G. Stuckenberg*, Gettysburg, 1987.
3. Richard A. Hoehn "J.H.W. Stuckenberg: American Lutheranism's First Social Ethicist" *Dialog* (Minnesota) 22, Winter 1983, 15-20.
4. Hoehn, *Dialog*, 17.
5. Stuckenberg Papers, Gettysburg College.
6. *A Shield and Hiding Place, The Religious Life of the Civil War Armies* by Gardiner H. Shattuck (Mercer University Press, 1987).
7. *Erie Weekly Gazette*, 11 September 1862.
8. U. S War Department, *The War of the Rebellion: A Compilation of the Official Record of the Union and Confederate Armies* [128 vols.; Washington, 1880-1901], i, XXI, 233.
9. John W. Busey and David G. Martin, *Regimental Strengths and Losses at Gettysburg*, (Highstown NJ: Longstreet House, 1986), 242.
10. "History of the 145th." manuscript, Stuckenberg Papers, Gettysburg College.
11. McCreary Collection, Box 9, File 3. Erie County Historical Society. Receipt for American Tract Society to Rev. J. H. W. Stuckenberg, November 20, 1864.

CHAPTER ONE

1. The First English Evangelical Lutheran Church of Erie, Pennsylvania, was founded August 15, 1861, with 41 charter members. The church was organized by members of St. John's German Lutheran Church in Erie, who felt a "need of an English Lutheran Church, in order that their families might enjoy a united church relation, because their children were receiving an English education and were in danger of drifting into any church but their own." In 1862 the congregation purchased a lot on the corner of Eleventh and Peach Streets, and by 1864 had erected a small frame structure. The Church remained in use until replaced by a more substantial brick edifice in 1887; that building is now called Luther Memorial Church. (*History of Luther Memorial Church, Erie Pennsylvania: 1861-1911* [np, nd {Erie, 1911?}], 5-6). The smaller German churches are still in existence: St. Peters is located outside of McKean and St. James is in Fairview.
2. Stuckenberg was supported by his congregation who described him as being a person of "good moral character, exemplary conduct, and untarnished reputation" (Evjen, 103-104). This view of Reverend Stuckenberg was affirmed by the *Erie Weekly Gazette* which stated: "Mr. S. is a talented young man, in prime of life, devotedly pious, and deeply interested in the religious work of sustaining a government which we are warranted to believe is a Divine ordinance" (*Erie Weekly Gazette*, 18 September 1862).
3. Company K, under the command of Captain John W. Walker, was not up to full strength when the rest of the regiment was mustered in and as a result missed the unit's departure on September 11. Company K was mustered into federal service on September 12, 1862.
4. Private Clark Dumars, Company K; discharged December 31, 1862. His discharge stated that he suffered from "temporary fits of insanity.... Should never have been enlisted" (Compiled Military Service Records (Union) 145th Pennsylvania Infantry, RG 94, National Archives, Washington D.C.).

5   Federal losses for Antietam were reported as 2,010 killed, 9,416 wounded, and 1,043 captured or missing, for a total 12,469. Confederate losses are harder to ascertain, but estimates for the period 14-20 September 1862 place Rebel casualties as 1,567 killed, 8,725 wounded, and 2,000 captured or missing for a probable loss of 12,292. (Jay Luvas and Harold W. Nelson, *The U. S. Army War College Guide to the Battle of Antietam: The Maryland Campaign of 1862* [Carlisle, Pennsylvania: South Mountain Press, 1987], 301-302).
6   The 111th Pennsylvania Volunteer Infantry Regiment, formed September 2, 1861, under the command of Colonel Matthew Schlaudecker, was composed of men from the northwestern counties of the state. At the Battle of Antietam, the regiment suffered its greatest losses during the war. Entering the field with thirteen officers and 230 men, the command suffered a loss of 115. (John Richards Boyle, *Soldiers True: The Story of the One Hundred and Eleventh Regiment Pennsylvania Veteran Volunteers and of its Campaigns in the War for the Union 1861-1865*, [New York: Eaton and Mains, 1903], 60-62, 65).
7   Christian Startzman, 1809-1880, had attended both the Gettysburg Lutheran Theological Seminary and Pennsylvania College of Gettysburg in 1837-38. (Clyde B. Stover and Charles W. Beachem, *The Alumni Record of Gettysburg College, 1832-1932* [Gettysburg: Gettysburg College, 1932], 475; and Abdel Ross Wentz, *Gettysburg Lutheran Theological Seminary Alumni Record* [Harrisburg: Evangelical Press, 1964], 12).
8   Captain Dyer Loomis, commanding Company C, and his son Private George Lamertine Loomis (Service Records, National Archives).
9   Lieutenant Colonel David Berkley McCreary, 1826-1906, was an educator and lawyer of note in pre-war Erie, and was a member of the elite pre-war milita known as the Wayne Guards. At the call for three month regiments in 1861, he joined Colonel John McLean's "Erie Regiment," serving as a Lieutenant under Captain Hiram L. Brown. Upon the regiment's expiration of service, he returned to Erie and helped in the recruitment and organization of the 145th Pennsylvania. Elected Lieutenant Colonel, he served with the regiment throughout the war, being taken prisoner twice: once along with over 100 of his command at Chancellorsville, and again at Petersburg. McCreary was breveted Brigadier General in 1865, and was mustered out with the regiment in June 1865. After the war he served as Adjutant General of Pennsylvania and as a state legislator (*Erie Daily Times*, 5 February 1906).
10 The Irish Brigade consisted of the 63rd, 69th, and 88th New York Volunteers—regiments composed of Irish-Americans and Irish immigrants from the New York City area. Due to high casualties the brigade was forced to accept replacement regiments of non-Irish composition like the 145th (*Historical Times Illustrated Encyclopedia of the Civil War* [New York: Harper and Row, 1986], 384-385).
11 Colonel Hiram Loomis Brown, 1832-1880. By profession a hotel keeper in Erie, Brown learned the art of soldiering by service in the field. A member of the Wayne Guard, he was appointed Captain in McLane's Erie Regiment in 1861. With the return of the regiment to Erie, he joined McLane in the newly forming 83rd Pennsylvania Volunteer Infantry Regiment, being appointed commander of Company I. Wounded at the Battle of Gaines Mill in June 1862, Brown was captured by Rebel forces while in the hospital and remained in their care until exchanged. Returning home to a hero's welcome, Brown's recuperation coincided with the raising of the 145th. Elected Colonel, Brown would be wounded three more times during the war, twice at Fredericksburg, and then at Gettysburg. While acting as Brigade Commander during the Battle of Spottsylvania Court House in 1864, Brown was captured and imprisoned until August 1864. Promoted to Brevet Brigadier General in 1865, he was forced to resign from the service due to ill health. The post-war years saw him in the positions

of County Sheriff and Collector of Customs for the port of Erie, a position he held when death occurred at the age of forty due to complications from his war wounds. (Samuel P. Bates, *Martial Deeds of Pennsylvania* [Philadelphia: T. H. Davis and Co. 1875], 748-752; *Nelson's Biographical Dictionary and Historical Reference Book of Erie County, Pa.* p. 209; A. M. Judson, *History of the Eighty-Third Regiment Pennsylvania Volunteers*. [Erie: B. H. F. Lynn, 1865] 21, 25, 134; *Erie Weekly Gazette*, 3 July 1862, 3 August 3 1863, 15 December 1864, 23 February 1865; *Erie Advertiser*, 27 November 1880; *Erie Weekly Dispatch*, 27 November 1880; *Erie Daily Times*, 11 September 1909, 21 December 1909; Service Records, National Archives).

12 Thomas Francis Meagher, 1832-1865, was an Irish revolutionary who fled to the United States in 1852. He settled in New York City and entered the legal profession. Outspoken and charismatic, he made a name for himself among the Irish in the city. During the war, Meagher raised an all Irish Brigade for Federal service. He served with the army of the Potomac from Bull Run to Chancellorsville, and after 1863 in various departments throughout the South, finally being appointed Territorial Secretary for Montana, a post he held on his death (*Historical Times Encyclopedia*, 438).

13 Reports of Meagher's drunkenness circulated after Antietam, but were never proven. In his after-action report Meagher described his exit from the field by claiming that his horse had been shot from under him, the fall of which caused his removal from the field. A prodigious drinker among an army of legendary imbibers, his fondness for the bottle led to his death on July 1, 1865, when in the throes of a drinking spree, Meagher fell from a steamboat near Fort Benton, and drowned (Stephen W. Sears, *The Landscape Turned Red: The Battle of Antietam*, [New York, 1983], 243-244. *Historical Times Encyclopedia*, 438. *Official Records*, i: XIX: 1, 293-295).

14 This regiment was the Non-Irish 29th Massachusetts Volunteer Infantry Regiment, which remained with the Irish Brigade until October 1862, when it was replaced by the 116th Pennsylvania Volunteers, a unit of heavy Irish composition (*Historical Times Encyclopedia*, 384).

15 Included in Stuckenberg's papers is a document listing many of the men who attended this service: "We the undersigned members of various Christian Denominations desiring to promote each others growth in Grace and Spiritual welfare generally, do hereby form ourselves into a regimental Church adopting the Bible as our only rule of Faith and Practice, and promising in whatever circumstances we may be to be faithful to our Christian Profession." There follows the signatures of 58 individuals, their denomination, and their residence. The ecumenical regimental congregation consisted of 28 Methodists, 12 Presbyterians, 6 Lutherans, 6 Baptists, 3 Episcopalians, 1 Congregationalist, and 1 Evangelical Alliance.

16 Captain William W. W. Wood, commanding Company G (Service Records, National Archives).

17 Stuart's Chambersburg Raid, October 9-13, 1862. 1,600 Confederate troopers under General J. E. B. Stuart raided behind Federal lines for the purpose of capturing badly needed remounts and disrupting supply and communication lines. During this raid Federal pursuit was nonexistent or ineffectual, enabling Stuart to repeat his celebrated ride around McClellan of June 1862. Recrossing the Potomac on October 12th, the Confederates returned without the loss of a single trooper, and with 1,200 captured horses (Emory Thomas, *Bold Dragoon: The Life of J.E.B. Stuart*, [New York, Harper and Row, 1986], 172-180; Burke Davis, *Jeb Stuart: The Last Cavalier*, [New York: Rinehart, 1957], 211-237; *Official Records*, i: XIX: 2, 52-56).

18 From William Cullen Bryant's poem "The Death of the Flowers."

19 First Lieutenant James F. Whittich, Company K, resigned his commission October 28, 1862 (Regimental Order Book, 145th Pennslyvania Infantry, Record Group 94, National Archives).
20 A type of maggot that infests meat.
21 On October 16-17, 1862, there was a reconnaissance up the Valley to Charles Town, Virginia (*Official Records*, i: XIX: 1: 2).
22 Private Henry Fidler, Company I, nineteen years old, and a member of Stuckenberg's Erie congregation (Service Records, National Archives. Membership Rolls of Luther Memorial Church, 1861. Luther Memorial Church, Erie, Pennsylavnia).
23 Second Lieutenant John B. Espy, Company H, recovered and continued to serve with the regiment (Service Records, National Archives).
24 First Lieutenant Ezra A. Parker, Company C, died at Harpers Ferry from Typhoid Fever (Service Records, National Archives. *Erie Observer*, 11 December 1862).
25 Most likely Thomas Babbington Macaulay, *Critical Historical and Miscellaneous Essays* (New York: A. C. Armstrong, 1860) and Immanuel Hermann Fichte, *Reden an die deutsche Nation* (Tubingen, 1859).
26 Colonel Samuel Thomas presented the state colors to the regiment on October 14, 1862, at Bolivar Heights (*Erie Daily Dispatch*, 1 November 1862; Richard A. Sauers, *Advance The Colors! Pennsylvania Civil War Battle Flags* [2 vols. Harrisburg: Capital Preservation Committee, 1991], II, 439).
27 This letter is not included in the collection at Gettysburg College. Letters dating from 1862-63 are almost non-existent. Karl Frederick Edward Stohlmann, 1810-1868, was a German Lutheran pastor who had both studied at Halle and served a parish in Erie from 1834-1838 (Jens Christian Roseland, *American Lutheran Biographies; or Historical Notices of Over Three Hundred and Fifty Leading Men of the American Lutheran Church From Its Establishment to the Year 1890*, [Milwaukee: A. Houtkamp and Son, 1890] 766-767).
28 The Stuckenberg Papers at Gettysburg College do not contain any letters from Elizabeth Ketchaus.
29 Private Albert. C. Richardson, Company A, deserted on November 1, 1862, and died at Allegheny Mountain, Pennsylvania on December 6, 1862 (Service Records, National Archives).
30 New Testament.
31 "What God does, he does well."
32 Private John Gorman, Company F (Service Records, National Archives).
33 Sentence fragments are rare in Stuckenberg's Diary. The few that do occur seem to come—like this—at moments of stress.
34 Captain Washington Brown, commanding Company I, would be wounded at Fredericksburg. He would not survive the amputation of his arm (Samuel P. Bates, *History of Pennsylvania Volunteers, 1861-5* [Harrisburg: B. Singerly, State Printer, 1869] IV, 545; Bates, *Martial Deeds*, 437-439; *Erie Weekly Gazette*, 25 December 1862, 1 January 1863).
35 First Lieutenant George G. Griswold, Company I, later assumed command of the company upon Captain Brown's death. He died July 17th, 1863, at Philadelphia due to complications arising from a wound received at Gettysburg (Bates, *Pennsylvania Volunteers*, IV, 545. *Erie Observer*, 16, 18, 23 July 1863).
36 Corporal William M. Brown, Company I, would later be promoted to sergeant, would be wounded at Gettysburg, would recover from his wound, would be transferred to the Veteran Reserve Corps, 124th Company, 2nd Battalion, and would be promoted to Second Lieutenant (Service Records, National Archives).
37 Second Lieutenant George A. Evans, Company I (Service Records, National Archives).

38 Private Daniel B. Farver, Company I, discharged due to wounds received at Fredericksburg (Service Records, National Archives).
39 Doctor George L. Potter, Regimental Surgeon (Service Records and Hospital Muster Rolls and Reports, National Archives).
40 Private Milton Ward, Company C (Service Records, National Archives).

CHAPTER TWO

1 Corporal John B. Fickinger, Company I, a member of Stuckenberg's Erie congregation. He was especially dear to the chaplain because of his strong desire to enter the ministry (Service Records, National Archives. Membership Roll, Luther Memorial Church).
2 Stuckenberg later expanded this anecdote: "I was kindly treated while at supper, which was late because the Union soldiers had disturbed them all afternoon, then one of the ladies asked my views of slavery. I gave her my opinion on the subject, when her eyes fairly flashed fire and the form of Venus suddenly assumed the aspect of Mars. She asked me whether I took the Bible for my guide? I was very hungry so I let her do all the talking whilst I did the eating" (J. H. W. Stuckenberg, "A History of the 145th Pennsylvania Volunteers," Stuckenberg Papers, Special Collections, Musselman Library, Gettysburg College, Pennsylvania).
3 Private Stacy Wilson, Chaplain of the 81st Pennsylvania Volunteers, a three month regiment (Bates, *Pennsylvania Volunteers*, III, 1173).
4 Captain James C. Hart.
5 Private George Lamertine Loomis' death from "camp fever" occurred at his home in North East, Pennsylvania. His sister, Mary, who cared for him, died a few weeks later of the same illness (*Erie Weekly Gazette*, 3 December 1862. Stuckenberg, "History of the 145th").
6 Private Stephen Bemis, Company I, died November 27, 1862, at Harpers Ferry (Service Records, National Archives).
7 Stuckenberg later described camp fever as "a kind of typhoid fever in an aggravated form, pneumonia and rheumatism being frequently connected with it . . . . It soon robs its victim of all energy, dispirits him and prostrates him . . . . The lips are parched and chapped; the tongue . . . is hard with a black crust . . . cracks reveal streaks of blood. A brown fluid at times fills and issues from the mouth . . . the whole body writhing and violently tossed from side to side. The effect on the mind is, however, worse than on the body. Reason often loses its throne and for days and even weeks the patient is delirious. The eyes are fixed, perhaps staring wildly; the lips move but no words are heard or the sentences are broken and incoherent; there seems to be an effort to communicate something, to relieve the mind of some burden; but in vain" (Stuckenberg, "History of the 145th").
8 James G. Payne, Regimental Quartermaster (Service Records, National Archives).
9 Major General Fitz John Porter Commanding the Fifth Corps, was relieved from duty and court martialed for disobedience and misconduct in the face of the enemy resulting from charges pressed by Major General John Pope, as part of the aftermath of the Second Battle of Bull Run. Porter was found guilty and discharged from the army on January 21, 1863. In 1878 he was exonerated of all charges. However, it was not until 1886 that he was restored to the rank of colonel (*Historical Times Encyclopedia*, 595).
10 At this point in the war Ambrose E. Burnside was in command of the Army of the Potomac (*Historical Times Encyclopedia*, 96-97).
11 Edinboro Normal School now Edinboro University of Pennsylvania, Edinboro (Erie County), Pennsylvania.
12 Corporal Edwin C. Sterrett, Company I, died at Falmouth, of typhoid fever (*Erie Observer*, 11 December 1862).
13 Private James A. Mowry, Company G (Service Records, National Archives).

14   Samuel M. Brown and Samuel W. Keefer, members of Stuckenberg's congregation. Brown died January 9, 1863 (Membership Roll, Luther Memorial Church).
15   Private Thomas Acock died at Falmouth December 5, 1862 (145th Regimental Hospital - Admissions, Deaths, National Archives).
16   Kimball H. Styles, Captain of Copmany F (Service Records, National Archives).
17   Private Henry W. Chellis, Company B (Regimental Hospital Book, National Archives).
18   Private Erastus Williams, Company D; Charles M. Lynch Captain of Company D (Descriptive Lists. Co's A thru K. 145th Pennsylvania Infantry, National Archives).
19   Private Virgil Crandall, Company B (Regimental Hospital Book, National Archives).

CHAPTER THREE

1   Stuckenberg is in error. General Sumner's Headquarters were located in Chatham, or the Lacy House on Stafford Heights, overlooking Fredericksburg. General Burnside's Headquarters were located in the Phillips house (Edwin C. Bearss, "Troop Movement Map - Battle of Fredericksburg," *Fredericksburg and Spotsylvania National Military Park*, nd, np).
2   In the early morning fog of December 11th, 1862, the Federal army attempted to lay pontoon bridges at three sites along the Rappahannock River. The upper crossing, directly in front of Fredericksburg, was strongly contested by Confederate forces in the town. Those forces held up the advance for most of the day, until driven from the town by Federal troops who crossed the river under fire and engaged in street fighting (*Official Records*, i: XXI, 87-89, 167-168, 181-183, 282-284, 578-579, 601-602).
3   Anna Maria Biest Stuckenberg. Letter not in Stuckenberg's papers.
4   Jane H. Clapperton of Edinburgh, Scotland. Stuckenberg met her during his 1859-61 stay in Germany. While other letters from Jane Clapperton are included in the Stuckenberg Collection, this particular letter is not present. Stuckenberg may have had great difficulty in reading this letter. The other Clapperton letters are written first in normal fashion on both sides of a sheet of very thin paper, then inverted and additional lines of text inserted in the spaces between the original lines. Some of the letters were also rotated ninety degrees and the process repeated.
5   Psalm 147:16.
6   Caroline Street.
7   Commodore Matthew Fontaine Maury, known as the "pathfinder of the seas," rented the house at 214 Lower Caroline Street (Fredericksburg Historical Museum, "Walk Through History: Lower Caroline Street").
8   First Lieutenant William H. Grant, Company B, continued to fight with a few men he was able to gather around him after the majority of the regiment had fled the field. He fired over 200 rounds at the Confederates behind the stonewall. His courageous action caught the attention of Brigadier General Hancock, who commended him to his commander. Lieutenant Grant died in Georgetown on July 14, 1863, from Pneumonia (*Erie Weekly Gazette*, 22 January 1863, 23 July 1863; Service Records, National Archives).
9   First Lieutenant John D. Black, Company F, promoted to Adjutant on May 13, 1863 (Service Records, National Archives).
10   Captain John W. Reynolds, Company A, was later wounded at Gettysburg, and promoted to Major on August 20th 1863. He was discharged by Special Order on September 19, 1863 (Service Records, National Archives. *Erie Weekly Gazette* 16 July 1863. *Erie Observer* 11 July 1863).
11   First Lieutenant Fletcher Clay, Company A, wounded in the head at Fredricksburg, December 13th, 1862. Lieutenant Clay's body was never identified (Letter to Lieutenant Long from Captain Reynolds, dated January 5th, 1863. Erie Historical Museum and Planetarium, Document Number: 6312:1).

12 Brigadier General William H. French, commander Third Division, Second Army Corps (*Historical Times Encyclopedia*, 292).
13 Stuckenberg quite clearly has had some time to think about what had occurred at Fredericksburg, had talked about it in a visit home [See Chapter 5] and had on February 9, 1863, composed a letter to the *Lutheran Observer* which was published on March 6, 1863. The sentiments expressed in this passage are more fully developed in that letter which is reproduced in Appendix I.
14 Private William D. Wicks, Company D (Quarterly Report of Deceased Soldiers of the 145th Regiment of Pennsylvania Volunteers for the quarter ending the thirty-first day of December 1862, National Archives).
15 Private Bryon E. Pierce, Company C (Service Records, National Archives. *Erie City Dispatch*, 25 December 1862).
16 First Lieutenant James H. Hamlin, Company I (Service Records, National Archives).
17 Private Daniel Farver, Company I (Service Records, National Archives).
18 Brigadier General John C. Caldwell, commander First Brigade, First Division, Second Army Corps. The performance of the 145th in their first battle did not please Caldwell, who stated in his after-action report: "The regiments, however, all behaved with the greatest gallantry and fought with steadiness, except the One hundred and forty-fifth Pennsylvania, which broke and fell back, its colonel being severely wounded" (*Official Records*, i: XXI, 233-234).
19 Corporal George Demond, of Company K, was an immigrant from Prussia. He had his left leg amputated above the knee (Service Records, National Archives; *Erie Weekly Gazette*, 25 December 1862).
20 Second Lieutenant Daniel Long, Company A, recovered and was promoted to First Lieutenant on January 13, 1863. He was discharged by Special Order on July 13th, 1863 (Service Records, National Archives).
21 First Lieutenant John H. Hubbard, Company D died at Falmouth, on December 16th, 1862 as a result of complications following his double amputation (Service Records, National Archives; *Erie Weekly Gazette*, 25 December 1862).
22 Second Lieutenant Charles H. Riblet, Company D (Service Records, National Archives. *Erie Weekly Gazette*, 25 December 1862, 19 March 1863).
23 2nd. Lt. Charles S. Carroll, Co. E (Carded Medical Records of Mexican and Civil War Volunteers, National Archives).
24 Captain William W. W. Wood, commander Company G, wounded in the left hip, died in Douglas Hospital in Washington D.C. on January 12, 1863 (Medical Records, National Archives. *Erie City Dispatch*, 27 December 1862).
25 Second Lieutenant John W. Vincent, Company G, wounded in shoulder, died January 8th, 1863 (Medical Records, National Archives. *Erie City Dispatch*, 27 December 1862).
26 Captain Andrew J. Mason, commander Company H, was wounded in the left leg and died January 12, 1863, in Washington D.C. from the result of complications from amputation. (Medical Records, National Archives; *Erie Weekly Gazette*, 25 December 1862, 22 January 1863; *Erie City Dispatch*, 27 December 1862).
27 Second Lieutenant Mavor R. Brown's body was returned to Erie by his father John S. Brown (Service Records, National Archives; *Erie Weekly Gazette*, 25 December 1862).
28 Private David D. King, Company E; though the Bible saved him from one wound, he was hit a second time in the leg and died as a result of that wound (Service Records, National Archives; *Erie City Dispatch*, 27 December 1862).
29 Stuckenberg must have kept some of these books and papers for himself. An 1873 letter from Maury's son Richard reads in part: "The house referred to in Fredericksburg was my father's. The books and papers now in your possession his. Should you still be in the mood for

I'm Surrounded by Methodists...

returning this property, they will reach their owner, if sent by express to this place." There is no indication as to the number, if any, of Maury's books and papers Stuckenberg retained. Only one fragment, signed by Richard Maury, remains in the collection. A pencil note in Stuckenberg's hand reads: "Dec 13, 1862" (Stuckenberg Papers).

30 Captain Martin L. Stultz, Company E (Bates, *Pennsylvania Volunteers*, IV, 535.)

CHAPTER FOUR

1 William Henry Channing, 1810-1884. Unitarian minister and Chaplain of the House of Representatives 1863-1864.

2 Captain John W. Walker left the regiment to become a paymaster in the U.S. Army with a promotion to the rank of major in January 1863 (Discriptive List: Co's A thru K, 145th Penna Inf., National Archives).

3 Private Robert W. Finn, Company D, wounded in the leg, died in Washington, D.C. on January 3, 1863 (*Erie Weekly Gazette*, 25 December 1862, 8 January 1863; Service Records, National Archives).

4 Reverend George A. Lyon, D. D., pastor of the First Presbyterian Church, Erie, September 29, 1829 until his death March 24, 1871 (*Erie City Directory 1854-1855*, [H. W. Hulbert, Publisher, Erie, 1854] 77; *Nelson's Biographical Dictionary and Historical Reference Book of Erie County, Pa.*, I, 438).

5 The *Erie Weekly Gazette* reported that Stuckenberg "feelingly narrated some of the incident of the terrible conflict and bore testimony to the dauntless courage and spirit of self-sacrifice of our soldiers" (*Erie Weekly Gazette*, 1 January 1863).

6 Henry Gingrich had been the spokesman for the group of Lutheran's who initially invited Stuckenberg to the Erie pastorate.

7 Sergeant Henry Skinner, Company D, died of wounds on December 16, 1862 (Service Records, National Archives; *Erie Weekly Gazette*, 8 January 1863).

8 From "The Death of the Virtuous" by Anna Letitia Barbauld, 1743-1835 (J. K. Hoyt, *Cyclopedia of Practical Quotations* [New York: Funk and Wagnells, 1896], p. 132).

9 One can only wonder if this "affectionate" farewell included Henry Gingrich's 13 year old daughter Mary; could it have been the start of the romance that would lead to the marriage of Stuckenberg and Mary Gingrich?

10 Mr. Henry Jareski, member of the church council, and Mr. Fredrick Ruess member of the congregation in Erie (*History of Luther Memorial Church*, 40).

11 Reverend John R. Hamilton of Fairview Presbyterian Church, Fairview, Pennsylvania, 1859-1864 (Church Records, Fairview Presbyterian Church, Fairview, Pennsylvania).

12 Clemet L. Vallandigham's infamous "Peace Speach" was given on January 14, 1863. John Armon Bingham was a member of the House of Representatives.

13 J. W. Alvord, Senior Secretary of the American Tract Society in October 1861 "entered upon the personal superintendence of the work of the Army of the Potomac and remained in the field until the close of the war" (Moss, 85).

14 Lieutenant Colonel McCreary, reported regimental losses as 238. Of which, 43 were killed, 152 wounded, and 43 prisoners or missing. This out of a total of 505 engaged. In closing his after-action report for Fredericksburg, he answered the slights of the regiment's actions by his superiors with simple facts: "Our state flag was pierced with eighteen bullets; our regimental flag with thirteen bullets and one large piece of railroad iron, whilst the flag-staff was shattered to pieces with a piece of shell. No words of mine are necessary to vindicate the bravery of the officers and men in this their first and at the same time most desperate battle of modern times; that is silently and triumphantly attested by the torn flags and shattered ranks now before me" (*Official Records*, i: XXI, 238-239).

15 Federal losses for the Battle of Fredericksburg were 1,284 killed, 9,600 wounded, and 1,769 prisoners or missing for an aggregate loss of 12,653. Confederate losses were reported as

595 killed, 4,061 wounded, 653 prisoners or missing (Thomas L. Livermore *Numbers and Losses in the Civil War in America: 1861-1865*, [Bloomington: Indiana University Press, 1957], 96).

CHAPTER FIVE

1 Private Marvin Callom, Company B, died April 13, 1863 at Falmouth (145th Regimental Hospital - Deaths, National Archives).
2 A nine month regiment raised in Dauphin and Lebanon Counties; it would have had numerous German speaking troops. The Regiment was at this time part of the Third Brigade of the Second Division, and was mustered out of service May 29, 1863 (Bates, *Pennsylvania Volunteers*, IV, 147-149).
3 T. R. Ewing, a "delegate" of the United States Christian Commission. The Christian Commission had been organized by the Y.M.C.A. to provide relief to the soilders at the front (Lemuel Moss, *Annals of the United States Christian Commission*, [Philadelphia: J. B. Lippincott, 1868], 150, 603).
4 Chaplain Stacey Wilson, 81st Pennsylvania (Bates, *Pennsylvania Volunteers*, II, 1173).
5 William Henry Stevens, of the Baltimore Conference of the Methodist Episcopal Church, pastor of the Bald Eagle Circut in Center, County, Pennsylvania, had been instrumental in the raising of part of Company H of the 148th in August 1862. He was appointed chaplain of the unit on September 7, 1862, and remained with the regiment until the end of the war (J. W. Muffly *The Story of our Regiment, A History of the 148th Pennsylvania Volunteers*, [Des Moines: Kenyon Printing, 1904], 191-227).
6 John C. Gregg, 127th Pennsylvania (Bates, *Pennsylvania Volunteers*, IV, 149).
7 F. A. Conwell, a Methodist minister from Minneapolis (John Q. Imholte, *The First Volunteers; history of the First Minnesota Volunteer Regiment, 1861-1865*, [Minneapolis: Ross and Haines 1963], 94).
8 Major General Joseph Hooker took command of the Army of the Potomac from Major General Ambrose Burnside on January 26, 1863 (*Historical Times Encyclopedia*, 370).
9 Colonel John Rutter Brooke, commanding the Fourth Brigade, First Division, Second Army Corps (Ezra J. Warner, *Generals in Blue*, [Baton Rouge: Louisiana State University, 1964], 46).
10 Christian Collection 5th Book.
11 Miss S. L. Olmstead was the Secretary of the Soldiers Aid Society in Erie. Chaplain Stuckenberg continued a regular correspondence with her concerning the supplies received and the morale of the regiment (*Erie Weekly Gazette*, 18 February 1863).
12 Brigadier General Oliver O. Howard, commanding Eleventh Army Corps (*Historical Times Encyclopedia*, 373).
13 Major General Edwin Vose Sumner died of pneumonia in Syracuse, New York on March 21, 1863, while on his way to his new assignment in the Department of Missouri (*Historical Times Encyclopedia*, 733).
14 John George Butler, 1826-1909, pastor of St. Paul's Lutheran Church, Washington D.C., 1849-73; Luther Place Memorial Church, Washington D. C., 1873-1909; Chaplain, U. S. House of Representatives 1869-1893; and Chaplain, U.S. Senate 1886-1893 (Wentz, 31).
15 A disease of horses in which the pastern (part of the foot) appears as if scratched.
16 On March 30, 1863, President Lincoln had issued a proclamation designating April 30 as "a day of national humiliation, fasting, and prayer." (Roy P. Basler, *Collected Works of Abraham Lincoln*, [New Brunswick, NJ: Rutgers University Press, 1953], VI, 155-156.) Stuckenberg had planned in advance for this service, and the prayer he had written is tipped in his copy of *A Liturgy for the Use of the Evangelical Lutheran Church* [Baltimore: Publication Rooms of the Evangelical Lutheran Church, 1847]. The complete text of the prayer is found in Appendix II.

17 Lieutenant Colonel McCreary and the soldiers of the regiment detailed to picket duty failed to get word of the withdrawal of the army; they held their position until: "An officer in gray stepped up from among the trees in the rear and demanded a surrender . . . McCreary declined, upon which the officer informed him that if he wished to fight the entire Confederate army he could be gratified, as they were then in possession of our position. Every tree in our rear gave up its many in gray. Resistance was useless and our men were marched to Richmond" (*Erie Weekly Gazette* 14 May 1863. Quote from Account told by McCreary to Mr. Moorhead as found in A. E. Caughey's *The Occasional Writings of Isaac Moorhead* [Erie, 1882] p. 133).

18 Moses W. Oliver, Company B (Descriptive List 145th Pennsylvania, National Archives).

19 First Lieutenant George F. C. Smart, Company G, was promoted to Captain in December 1864. He was captured a second time at Petersburg on 16 June 1864. Once again he survived imprisonment and was mustered out with his company in May 1865 (Service Records, National Archives).

20 First Lieutenant C. W. Deveraux, Company K, promoted to Captain in January 1864, and killed on May 12th, 1864, at the Battle of Spotsylvania Court House (Carded Medical Records, National Archives; *Erie Weekly Gazette*, 19 May 1864).

21 Second Lieutenant Hugh R. Stewart, Company H, promoted to First Lieutenant in April 1864; wounded in the assault on Petersburg on he was discharged by Special Order on August 22, 1864 (Service Records, National Archives).

22 The 113 officers and men captured at Chancellorsville came from Companies B, E, F, G, H, and K (*Erie Weekly Gazette*, 14 May 1863; *Erie Observer*, 16 May 1863).

23 Private Philemon Clark, Company F, was shot through the head and died May 3 (Carded Medical Records, National Archives; *Erie Observer*, 16 May 1863).

24 Major John W. Patton died of his wound (Carded Medical Records, National Archives).

25 The Chancellor Tavern.

26 Major General Darius N. Couch, commanding Second Army Corps (*Historical Times Encyclopedia*, 187).

27 L. H. Mitchell, a school teacher from Davenport, Iowa; after the war he pursued graduate study in Europe, and worked as an engineer in Egypt (Evjin ,72).

28 Private Samuel B. Weidler, Company A (Descriptive List 145th Pennsylvania, National Archives).

CHAPTER SIX

1 Herman Heinrich Stuckenberg.

2 Mrs. M. C. Keefer (*History of Luther Memorial Church*; "Parish Register of the First English Evangelical Lutheran Church" [Luther Memorial Church, Erie Pennsylvania], 6).

3 The term Copperhead was applied to the Peace Democrats of the North, who felt more conciliatory towards the South than did their Republican bretheran. Because members sometimes wore copper pennies as identification badges the nickname "copperhead" was applied (*Historical Times Encyclopedia*, 564).

4 In a letter to Mr. I. B. Gara, Editor of the *Erie Gazette*, Chaplain Stuckenberg wrote: "It (the gift) will serve to attach me still more firmly to the Regiment, for I now know that my attachment is reciprocated; it will encourage me in my labors and assure me that they are appreciated. If any success has attended my efforts, it is to a great extent due to the moral and religious character and the co-operation of those with and for whom I have been laboring, who without exception received me kindly and treated with respect the message I brought them. For this token of esteem and affection I feel a gratitude I cannot express. That it is sincere and lasting, I trust that the future will show" (*Erie Weekly Gazette*, 9 June 1863).

5   Berea Church, small Methodist Church on road running to Stafford Court House.
6   Chaplain Stuckenberg reflected on the severity and urgency of the march to Gettysburg in a lecture he gave in Warren, Pennsylvania, on January 6th, 1864:

> The march from the Rapphannock to Gettysburg was very severe, old soldiers declaring that it was the severest they had ever made. The weather was intensely hot, the sun pouring his burning rays upon that barren region of Virginia, as on a desert. Cases of sunstroke were common. Water was often scarce, and generally very poor. The roads were so dusty that at times the column in our immediate front could not be seen; and great clouds of dust were seen in the West, where Lee's army was marching. Blankets and tents and overcoats and all articles of clothing except what the soldiers wore, were thrown away, sometimes covering the road, sometimes gathered in heaps and burned, lest they should fall into the hands of the enemy. The ambulances were crowded everyday and numbers asked for admittance who were refused. Those that gave out were afraid to stop and rest because they were in great danger of being taken by the rebels. So they dragged their sick bodies and weary, sore limbs, along until they fell by the road side, panting for breath, some (conscious) others on the point of death and all suffering terribly. Brooks had to be waded, where men had not the time to take off their shoes which filled with water, then with dust and gravel, making their feet tender and in many cases covering them with blisters. Sometimes we were up and off very early in the morning; at others we marched till one, two, or three o'clock at night. Horses and mules fell dead in the road. Our Col's dog gave out and was left; but the men with their loads had to march on. Two days before the battle our corps marched through the heat and dust and brooks, up and down hill over 30 miles (J. H. W. Stuckenberg, "Warren Lecture," Stuckenberg Collection).

7   Major General Samuel Peter Heintzelman, removed from Corps command after the Second Battle of Bull Run, he was at this point in the war in command of portions of the forces defending Washington (*Historical Times Encyclopedia*, 356).
8   Brigadier Philip Kearney, killed September 1, 1862, at the Battle of Chantilly, Virginia (*Historical Times Encyclopedia*, 408-409).
9   Groveton.
10 Major General Franz Sigel.
11 A hot dry violent desert wind.
12 Thoroughfare Gap, Virginia, located on State Route 55 was described by General James Longstreet: "Its mean width is eighty yards. Its faces of basaltic rock rise in vertical ascent from one hundred to three hundred feet." Broad Run Creek flows through the gap, falling 1,300 feet, and providing power for the local mill. The mill still stands today (James Longstreet, *From Manassas to Appomattox* [Philadelphia: Lippincott, 1903], 174).
13 George Diehl 1814-1891, Lutheran Pastor in Frederick. Diehl was also an Associate Editor of *The Lutheran Observer*, a church journal that had in March 1863 published Stuckeberg's article "The Effects of a Battle on a Man's Religious Views and Beliefs." Stuckenberg contributed more than one hundred articles to this journal (Wentz, 14; Hoehn, 89-94).
14 Theophilus Stork, 1814-1874, influential Lutheran pastor in Baltimore. Stork had three sons: Charles, William, and Theophilus (Stover, 4).
15 Major General George G. Meade, replaced Major General Joseph Hooker on June 28, 1863, as commander of the Army of the Potomac. Upon later reflection Stuckenberg wrote:

> "On Sunday the 28th of June, four days before the battle, while the army was at Frederick Md. Gen. Hooker was relieved of his command. He was a gallant officer, daring and spirited. Soon after his appointment, he excited the greatest enthusiasm and won the unbounded confidence of the army, till the battle of Chancellorsville created mistrust. He was emphatically an active general good at execution where another planned. He made the

cavalry efficient and provided for his troops, as perhaps no other general has done.... Hooker failed at Chancellorsville, when he ought to have succeeded; but what he can do with a smaller force was demonstrated at Williamsburgh, at Antietam and Lookout Mountain.... Of General Meade the vast majority knew nothing, except that he had been the commander of the 5th Corps. He was the hero of no battle, and his appointment excited neither enthusiasm nor confidence. His exterior was cold, his manner uninviting. Only four days before the battle he was appointed to the command of the army.... His appointment seemed to be a desperate experiment in a desperate emergency (Stuckenberg, "Warren Lecture").
16   First Lieutenant Horatio F. Lewis, Company D (Service Records, National Archives).
17   Dr. Daniel W. Richards, assistant surgeon of the 145th.
18   Levi T. Williams 1814-1887, Lutheran Pastor in Taneytown, Maryland, 1858-67 (Wentz, 22).
19   Major General John F. Reynolds.

CHAPTER SEVEN
1   The Irish Brigade Service of Absolution was conducted by Chaplain Father William Corby. The sight of this event touched all who saw it. Major St. Clair A. Mulholland, of the 116th Pennsylvania Volunteers, later recalled that the "scene was more than impressive, it was awe inspiring" (*Pennsylvania at Gettysburg: Ceremonies at the Dedication of the Monuments*, [Harrisburg: W. S. Ray, 1904], II, 623).
2   Brigider General Samuel K. Zook, commanding Third Brigade, First Division, Second Army Corps, was shot in the abdomen and died on July 3rd, 1863 (Pfanz, Harry W., *Gettysburg: the Second Day* [Chapel Hill: University of North Carolina Press, 1987], 277).
3   Most likely the George Spangler Farm (Gregory A. Coco, *A Vast Sea of Misery: A history and guide to the Union and Confederate Field Hospitals at Gettysburg July 1 - November 20, 1863* [Gettysburg: Thomas Publications, 1988], 105-107).
4   J. S. Whillden, Assistant Regimental Surgeon. Later promoted to Surgeon with the 208th Pennsylvania Volunteers (Service Records, National Archives).
5   Mistaken company designation of Private Frank M. Forbes, Company I, wounded through the right lung 2 July 1863 (*Erie Weekly Gazette*, 16 July 1863; Carded Medical Records, National Archives).
6   Private Erastus Allen, Company I, died of wounds, July 4, 1863, and is buried in Gettysburg National Cemetery. During the Chancellorsville Campaign, Private Allen's courage under fire was noted in Colonel Brown's after-action report. "I cannot close this report without referring to the gallant conduct of Private Erastus A. Allen, of Company I, who, while engaged in the fight on Sunday, volunteered to carry cartridges to the men of the Sixty-fourth New York Volunteers, who were destitute of ammunition and could not procure any. . . . [He] succeeded in doing so, although exposed to a heavy fire in the undertaking" (*Official Records*, i: XXV: I, 349).
7   Major General George W. Slocum, Commanding Twelfth Corps.
8   Private Harrison H. Hays was left behind sick at Gettysburg after the regiment moved out. Hays died on September 15, 1863 (Service Records, National Archives).
9   Brigadier General John Gibbons, commanding Second Division, Second Corps.
10 Captain John C. Hilton, Commanding Company K, recovered and was promoted to Brevet Major on March 13, 1865. He was present at the dedication of the 145th's Monument at Gettysburg in 1889. Shortly after Stuckenberg's death he wrote of his experience in the field hospital: "the enemies shell came screeching and crashing through the trees—it became necessary to hastily remove back to a safer position. When they came to me I refused to allow them to remove me, as I was told I could not live and by this time I was in excruciating pain; and for an hour or two I remained alone, when the Capt[ain] came back with four stalwart

men and pointed me out, and without paying any attention to my remonstrations, raised my stretcher, and 'taking step' hurried me to the rear amid the bursting of shells." Captain Hilton's wound is graphically described in *The Medical and Surgical History of the War of the Rebellion* [Washington: GPO, 1883], part III, vol. II, p. 273. (*Pennsylvania At Gettysburg*, II, 700-702); Quotation from letter of John C. Hilton to Mrs. J. H. W. Stuckenberg, 7 June 1906 [Stuckenberg Collection].

11 After the wounding of Colonel Brown, Captain Reynolds took command of the regiment and led it into the Wheatfield, during which he was slightly wounded in the head; upon the withdrawal of the regiment from the area, he turned over command to Captain Moses Oliver. With many of the regiment's officers out of action, Stuckenberg took over many of the administrative duties of including writing a summary of the unit's action for Lieutenant Hatch, assistant adjutant general of the 4th Brigade. The after-action report and this diary paragraph are remarkably similar (Stuckenberg: "After-Action Report on Gettysburg." [Photocopy from Gettysburg National Military Park, original in Record Group 54, National Archives]).

12 Private H. L. Talmadge, Company I (*Erie Weekly Gazette*, 18 July 1863; *Erie Observer*, 11 July 1863; Service Records, National Archives).

13 1st Sergeant James D. Cochran, Company C (*Erie Weekly Gazette*, 16 July 1863; Service Records, National Archives).

14 Corporal J. Milton Taylor, Company B (*Erie Weekly Gazette*, 18 July 1863; Service Records, National Archives).

15 Private Joseph Marsh, Company B (*Erie Weekly Gazette*, 18 July 1863; Service Records, National Archives).

16 Private Ira Corbin, Company D (*Erie Weekly Gazette*, 18 July 1863; Service Records, National Archives).

17 Major L. W. Bradley, Major Commanding the 64th N.Y. Volunteers recorded in his after-action reports that "On the 4th we buried our dead and held short religious services conducted by Chaplain John H. W. Stuckenberg, of the one hundred and forty-fifth Pennsylvania Volunteers" (*Official Records*, i: XXVII: I: 406-407).

18 Lieutenant George H. FInch, Company E, died of his wounds on July 6, 1863 (Service Records, National Archives).

19 Private Lewis Stallman, Company I (Service Records, National Archives).

20 Corporal Horace Mann, Company I, wounded in thigh, recovered from his wound (*Erie Weekly Gazette*, 18 July 1863; *Erie Observer*, 11 July 1863; Service Records, National Archives).

21 Samuel Henry, 1828-1910, Lutheran pastor in Littlestown, Pennsylvania, 1858-68 (Wentz, 33).

22 Stuckenberg has confused the names of two colleges with the location of one. In 1850 Franklin College located in Lancaster, Pennsylvania, and Marshall College located in Mercersburg, Pennsylvania, had been consolidated into Franklin and Marshall College in Lancaster (Charles A. Glatfelter, *A Salutary Influence: Gettysburg College, 1832-1985* [Gettysburg: Gettysburg College, 1987], 75).

23 First Lieutenant Horatio F. Lewis, Company D had been promoted from Sergeant Major to First Lieutenant on December 13th, 1863 (Bates, *Pennsylvania Volunteers*, IV, 532; *Erie Weekly Gazette*, 18 July 1863; Service Records, National Archives).

24 Second Lieutenant Jeremiah Birtcil, Company F was wounded in the right arm (Bates, *Pennsylvania Volunteers*, IV, 537; *Erie Weekly Gazette*, 16 July 1863; *Erie Observer*, 11 July 1863; Service Records, National Archives).

25 Stuckenberg left space for a date, but did not fill it in later.

26 Martin Luther Stover, 1820-1870, Professor of History and Latin Language and Literature, was one of the leading good Samaritans in Gettysburg after the battle (Glatfelter, I, 186).

27 Henry L. Baugher, 1804-1868, President of Pennsylvania (Gettysburg) College, 1850-1868.

CHAPTER EIGHT

1 George Augustus Nixdorff, 1823-1907, Lutheran pastor in Burkittsville, Maryland, 1858-1866 (Wentz, 28).
2 First Lieutenant George T. Jewett, Company C (Bates, Carded Medical Records, National Archives).
3 Doctor Francis Reynolds, Surgeon of 88th New York Volunteers (D. P. Conyngham, *The Irish Brigade and its Campaigns With Some Account of the Corcoran Legion, and Sketches of the Principal Officers* [New York: William McSorley, 1867], 559).
4 Keedysville.
5 Major General William Henry French in charge of the District of Harpers Ferry during the Gettysburg Campaign. Succeeded Sickles as commander of III Corps (Warner, 161-162).
6 Key's Gap located about three miles south of Harpers Ferry.
7 The *Erie Gazette* reported McCreary's return from Libby Prison in Richmond to Erie on 4 June 1863. After exchange McCreary reported back to the regiment. Reynolds, recovered somewhat from his Gettysburg wound, also rejoined the regiment (*Erie Observer*, 16 May 1863; *Erie Weekly Gazette*, 4 June 1863, 16 July 1863).
8 Lieutenant Melvin H. Bemis, Company C, was arrested for being absent without leave from the U. S. General Hospital at Georgetown. Tried on August 14, 1863, Lieutenant Bemis was found guilty; his sentence was forfeiture of all pay and allowances for three months, and a public reprimand in General Orders. The reprimand was remitted, and Bemis was discharged in January 1865 on a surgeons certificate (Service Records, National Archives).
9 Brigadier General William Hays. A brigade commander in the 1st Division of the II Corps during the Battle of Chacellorsville, Hays was taken prisoner on the 3rd of May 1863. Exchanged shortly after his capture, he returned to the army just before the beginning of the Gettysburg Campaign. When Generals Hancock and Gibbon were wounded command of the II Corps was given to him. Hays retained this command until September 13, 1863 (Warner, 224-225).
10 Colonel John Singleton Mosby, commander of the Partisan Rangers which so terrorized the Federal forces in this area of Virginia (*Historical Times Encyclopedia*, 524).
11 Seymour D. Ware, Hospital Steward, somehow later returned to the unit and was present when the unit was mustered out of service (Muster Rolls of the Hospital Department, National Archives).
12 Major S. Octavius Bull, 53rd Pennsylvania (Francis A. Walker, *History of the Second Army Corps in the Army of the Potomac* [New York: C. Scribner's Sons, 1886], 406; Bates, *Pennsylvania Volunteers*, II, 98).
13 Major General Alfred Pleasonton in command of the Cavalry Corps (Warner, 373-374).
14 Major General William "Extra Billy" Smith, CSA. Nicknamed "Extra Billy" for the extra payments he received from the Post Office Department for mileage covered while owner of a pre-war mail-coach service. Smith had served in the State Senate, five terms in the U.S. House of Representatives, and one term as Governor of Virginia. Noted for his valor on the field, he rose to the rank of Major General (*Historical Times Encyclopedia*, 698).
15 Brigadier General Gouverneur Kemble Warren, Chief Engineer of the Army of the Potomac (*Historical Times Encyclopedia*, 803).
16 George W. Martin, John Richard Martin, and Robert E. Martin of Company H of the 4th Virginia Cavalry (Kenneth L. Stiles, *4th Virginia Cavalry* [Lynchburg: H. E. Howard, 1985], 124).

CHAPTER NINE

1 Elk Run, about 6 miles east of Bealton.
2 *Leisure Hours in Town* by Andrew Kennedy Hutchison Boyd, Boston, Ticknor and Fields, 1862 was reprinted several times over the next two decades. Some of the topics included "Concerning the parson's leisure hours in town;" "Concerning veal;" "Concerning people of whom more might have been made."
3 The Christian Commission tent, large enough to hold 200 men, had been erected at Bealton on August 10 (Moss, 401).
4 Mrs. John Harris, secretary of the Ladies Aid Society of Philadelphia, one of many women who attempted to provide aid and comfort to the sick and wounded (Frank Moore, *Women of the War; their heroism and self-sacrifice* [Hartford: S. S. Scranton, 1866], 176-212).
5 Dorothea Dix. Nurse and hospital reformer with total authority over selection and managment of all women nurses (*Historical Times Encyclopedia*, 222).
6 The order admitting Stuckenberg to Seminary Hospital is contained in Stuckenberg's file at the National Archives. The physicians who signed this order are: Robert O. Abbott, William Radcliffe Dewitt Jr., Meredith Clymer, and Andrew Flint Shelton (Service Records, National Archives; *The Medical and Surgical History of the Civil War* [Wilmington, NC: Broadfoot Publishing Company, 1992], Index, vol. 1, pp. 1, 16, 21, and 68).
7 The Seminary Hospital consisted of a four story brick building that had been occupied as a young ladies' seminary. Ward 1 located on the first floor was the largest room in the building. A floor-plan of this hospital is included *Medical and Surgical History* (*Medical and Surgical History*, 1992, VI, 899-900).
8 Probably Peter Wise, Company I, 163rd Pennsylvania, who was discharged on a Surgeon's certificate August 27, 1863 (Bates, *Pennsylvania Volunteers*, IV, 1069).
9 I.e., the talk turned to chaplains.
10 William F. Hill, 20th Massachusetts; and John Smith, 1st Company, Massachusetts Sharpshooters (Robert I. Alotta, *Civil War Justice: Union Army Executions Under Lincoln* [Shippensburg, Pennsylvania: White Mane Publishing, 1989], 76-77).
11 Jesse Mayberry, 71st Pennsylvania (John Day Smith, *The History of the Nineteenth Regiment of Maine Volunteer Infantry 1862-1865* [Minneapolis: Great Western Printing Company, 1909], 103).
12 Stuckenberg was obviously quite affected by this execution. In most cases there are few sentence fragments, additions between lines, or words crossed out in his journal. This passage displays more errors of this sort than other pages of the journal.
13 As usual in war the initial reports may tend to be overly euphoric. Battery Wagner was not abandoned until shortly before a scheduled Union Attack on September 7. Fort Sumter held out until abandoned by the Confederates on 17 February 1865 (John Stewart Bowman, *The Civil War Almanac* [New York: Facts on File, 1982], 166-167; and Chris Bishop, *1400 Days: the Civil War Day by Day* [New York: Gallery Books, 1990], 224).
14 Epsom salts.
15 Probable identification: Private John Joseph Gazza, Company I, drafted at Philadelphia, Pennsylvania, on June 17, 1863. An engineer, and a native of Mexico, Private Gazza deserted on September 16th, 1863, at Culpepper, Virginia (Descriptive List of Deserters: 145th Pennsylvania Regiment, Provost's Marshall's Office, National Archives).
16 Probable identification: Martin Holtz of Company K was a 63 year old German immigrant who entered the regiment in September 1863 and was discharged in December 1863.
17 So it is with me.
18 Gideon Welles, Secretary of the Navy.

19 The physical descriptions of the drafted men do not indicate that one of the men was six feet five inches tall. Three men were listed as being six feet two inches tall (Descriptive Book, National Archives).
20 Private Charles Baker, Company A, draftee, reported to regiment on August 22, 1863, died September 9th, 1863, at Morrisville, Virginia (Carded Medical Records, National Archives).
21 The incumbent Republican Governor, Andrew Gregg Curtin, defeated the Democrat challenger, Judge George W. Woodward 269, 506 to 254, 171. (*The Pennsylvania Manual 1972-1974* [Harrisburg, 1974]).
22 Carded Military Records, National Archives.

APPENDIX TWO

1 This manuscript was inserted is Stuckenberg's copy of *A Liturgy for the Use of the Evangelical Lutheran Church*, Baltimore, 1847.

BIBLIOGRAPHY

This bibliography is neither comprehensive nor critical. It is quite simply a listing of the works used to directly annotate Stuckenberg's Diary. Many eminent scholars have written on each of the engagements in which the 145th Pennsylvania participated. Those works were indispensable in our work—but most of those titles are not cited here.

The National Archives and Records Administration holdings are vital to a work such as this. The fine work by Kenneth Munden and Henry Beers, *The Union: A guide to federal archives relating to the Civil War*, [Washington, 1982] led us to the records of the 145th Pennsylvania. Both the Erie County Historical Society and the Erie Museum and Planetarium have material related to individuals in the 145th scattered throughout their collections. The Stuckenberg Papers in Special Collections, Musselman Library, Gettysburg College were indispensable to the editors. The original parish records of Luther Memorial Church are still maintained by the congregation.

Alotta, I. Robert. *Civil War Justice: Union Army Executions Under Lincoln.* Shippensburg, PA: White Mane Publishing, 1989.

Boyle, John Richards. *Soldiers True: The Story of the One Hundred and Eleventh Regiment Pennsylvania Veteran Volunteers and of its Campaigns in the War for the Union 1861-1865.* New York: Eaton and Mains, 1903.

Basler, Roy P. *Collected Works of Abraham Lincoln*, 9 vols. New Brunswick, NJ: Rutgers University Press, 1953.

Bates, Samuel P. *History of Pennsylvania Volunteers, 1861-5*, 5 vols. Harrisburg: B. Singerly, State Printer, 1869.

---. *Martial Deeds of Pennsylvania.* Philadelphia: T. H. Davis and Co., 1875.

Bishop, Chris. *1400 Days: the Civil War Day by Day.* New York: Gallery Books, 1990.

Bowman, John Stewart. *The Civil War Almanac.* New York: Facts on File, 1982.

Busey, John W., and David G. Martin. *Regimental Strengths and Losses at Gettysburg.* Highstown, NJ: Longstreet House, 1986.

Caughey, A. E. *The Occasional Writings of Isaac Moorhead.* Erie: A. E. Caughey, 1882.

Coco, Gregory A. *A Vast Sea of Misery: A history and guide to the Union and Confederate Field Hospitals at Gettysburg July 1 - November 20, 1863.* Gettysburg: Thomas Publications, 1988.

Conyngham, D. P. *The Irish Brigade and its Campaigns With Some Account of the Corcoran Legion, and Sketches of the Principal Officers.* New York: William McSorley, 1867.

Davis, Burke. *Jeb Stuart: The Last Cavalier.* New York: Rinehart, 1957.
Erie Advertiser. 27 November 1880.
Erie City Directory 1854-1855. Erie, Pennsylvania: H. W. Hulbert, 1854.
Erie City Dispatch. 1 November, 25, 27 December 1862.
Erie Daily Times. 5 February 1906, 11 September 1909, 21 December 1909.
Erie Observer. 11 December 1862, 16 May 1863, 11, 16, 18, 23 July 1863.
Erie Weekly Dispatch. 27 November 1880.
Erie Weekly Gazette. 11, 18 September 1862; 3, 25 December 1862; 1, 22 January 1863; 18, 23 February 1863; 19 March 1863; 14 May 1863; 3 July 1863; 3 August 1863; 19 May 1864; 15 December 1864; 23 February 1865.
Evjen, J. O. *The Life of J. H. W. Stuckenberg.* Minneapolis: Lutheran Free Church Publishing Company, 1938.
Glatfelter, Charles A. *A Salutary Influence: Gettysburg College, 1832-1985.* Gettysburg: Gettysburg College, 1987.
Historical Times Illustrated Encyclopedia of the Civil War. New York: Harper and Row, 1986.
History of Luther Memorial Church, Erie Pennsylvania: 1861-1911. Erie: Luther Memorial Church, 1911[?].
Hoehn, Richard A. *Now We See Through A Glass Darkly—But We See: The Papers of J. H. W. and Mary G. Stuckenberg.* Gettysburg: Musselman Library, Gettysburg College, 1987.
---. "J. H. W. Stuckenberg: American Lutheranism's First Social Ethicist." Dialog (Minnesota) 22 (Winter 1983): 15-20.
---. "The Letters of Mary and Wilburn." *Lutheran Women* XX, 4 (May 1982): 3-7.
Honeywell, Roy J. *Chaplains of the United States Army.* Washington: GPO, 1958.
Hoyt, J. K. *Cyclopedia of Practical Quotations.* New York: Funk and Wagnalls, 1896.
Imholte, John Q. *The First Volunteers; history of the First Minnesota Volunteer Regiment, 1861-1865.* Minneapolis: Ross and Haines, 1963.
Judson, A. M. *History of the Eighty-Third Regiment Pennsylvania Volunteers.* Erie: B. H. F. Lynn, 1865.
A Liturgy for the Use of the Evangelical Lutheran Church. Baltimore: Publication Rooms of the Evangelical Lutheran Church, 1847.
Livermore, Thomas L. *Numbers and Losses in the Civil War in America: 1861-1865.* Bloomington: Indiana University Press, 1957.
Longstreet, James. *From Manassas to Appomattox.* Philadelphia: Lippincott, 1903.
Luvas, Jay and Harold W. Nelson. *The U. S. Army War College Guide to the Battle of Antietam: The Maryland Campaign of 1862.* Carlisle, PA: South Mountain Press, 1987.
The Medical and Surgical History of the Civil War, 15 vols. Wilmington, NC: Broadfoot Publishing Company, 1992.
The Medical and Surgical History of the War of the Rebellion, 6 vols. Washington: Government Printing Office, 1883.

Moore, Frank. *Women of the War: their heroism and self-sacrifice.* Hartford: S. S. Scranton, 1866.

Moss, Lemuel. *Annals of the United States Christian Commission.* Philadelphia: J. B. Lippincott, 1868.

Muffly, J. W. *The Story of our Regiment, A History of the 148th Pennsylvania Volunteers.* Des Moines: Kenyon Printing, 1904.

Nelson's Biographical Dictionary and Historical Reference Book of Erie County, Pa. Erie: S. B. Nelson, 1896.

The Official Military Atlas of the Civil War. New York: Fairfax Press, 1983. (Reprint of *Atlas to Accompany the Official Records of the Union and Confederate Armies*: Washington, GPO, 1891-1895).

Pennsylvania at Gettysburg: Ceremonies at the Dedication of the Monuments. Harrisburg: W. S. Ray, 1904.

Pfanz, Harry W. *Gettysburg: the Second Day.* Chapel Hill: University of North Carolina, 1987.

Roseland, Jens Christian. *American Lutheran Biographies; or Historical Notices of Over Three Hundred and Fifty Leading Men of the American Lutheran Church From Its Establishment to the Year 1890.* Milwaukee: A. Houtkamp and Son, 1890.

Sauers, Richard A. *Advance The Colors! Pennsylvania Civil War Battle Flags*, 2 vols. Harrisburg: Capital Preservation Committee, 1991.

Sears, Stephen W. *The Landscape Turned Red: The Battle of Antietam.* New Haven: Ticknor and Fields, 1983.

Schenck, J. S. *History of Warren County, Pennsylvania, with illustrations and biographical sketches of some of its prominent men and pioneers.* Syracuse: D. Mason and Company, 1887.

Shattuck, Gardiner H. *A Shield and Hiding Place, The Religious Life of the Civil War Armies.* Macon, GA: Mercer University Press, 1987.

Stiles, Kenneth L. *4th Virginia Cavalry.* Lynchburg: H. E. Howard, 1985.

Stover, Clyde B. and Charles W. Beachem. *The Alumni Record of Gettysburg College, 1832-1932.* Gettysburg: Gettysburg College, 1932.

Stuckenberg, J. H. W. "The Effects of A Battle on a Man's Religious Views and Beliefs." *Lutheran Observer* 34, no. (March 6, 1863).

---. "A History of the 145th Pennsylvania Volunteers", Stuckenberg Papers, Special Collections, Musselman Library, Gettysburg College, Pennsylvania.

Thomas, Emory. *Bold Dragoon: The Life of J.E.B. Stuart.* New York, Harper and Row, 1986.

U. S. War Department. *The War of the Rebellion: A Compilation of the Official Record of the Union and Confederate Armies*, 128 vols. Washington: Government Printing Office, 1880-1901.

Walker, Francis A. *History of the Second Army Corps in the Army of the Potomac.* New York: C. Scribner's Sons, 1886.

Warner, Ezra J. *Generals in Blue.* Baton Rouge: Louisiana State University, 1964.

Wentz, Abdel Ross. *Gettysburg Lutheran Theological Seminary Alumni Record.* Harrisburg: Evangelical Press, 1964.

---. *History of the Evangelical Lutheran Church of Frederick, Maryland 1738-1938.* Harrisburg: Evangelical Press, 1938.

INDEX

Abbott, Robert O., 102
Acock, Mrs., 47
Acock, Thomas, 36
Allen, Erastus, 79, 83
Alvord, J. W., 52, 56
Baker, Charles, 113
Baugher, Henry L., 87
Bemis, Melvin H., 93
Bemis, Stephen, 29
Bingham, John Armon, 52
Birtcil, Jeremiah, 85
Black, John D., 40, 46, 59, 78, 79, 84
Boyd, Andrew Kennedy Hutchison, 102
Bradley, L. W., 83
Brooke, John Rutter, 59, 77, 95, 96, 105
Brown, Hiram Loomis, 5, 14, 19, 38, 40, 41, 44, 47, 52, 69, 77, 78
Brown, John, 4, 49, 92
Brown, John S., 48
Brown, Mavor R., 44
Brown, Samuel M., 36, 50, 51
Brown, Washington, 24, 44, 49, 70
Brown, William M., 24, 27, 43, 81, 83
Bull, S. Octavius, 97
Burnside, Ambrose E., 33, 53
Butler, John George, 59
Caldwell, John C., 5, 44, 57, 89, 90, 93
Carroll, Charles S., 44, 46
Channing, William Henry, 48
Chellis, Henry W., 36
Clapperton, Jane H., 38
Clark, Philemon C., 64
Clay, Fletcher, 40, 41, 44, 95
Clymer, Meredith, 103
Cochran, James D., 81
Collom, Marvin, 56
Conwell, F. A., 56
Corbin, Ira, 81
Couch, Darius N., 65, 66
Curtin, Andrew Gregg, 5, 113
Demond, George, 44
Devereaux, C. W., 64
DeWitt, William Radcliffe, Jr., 103
Diehl, George, 75, 88
Dix, Dorothy, 102
Dumars, Clark, 11

Espy, John B., 18
Evans, George A., 24, 34
Evjen, John O., 1
Ewing, T. R., 56, 57
Farver, Daniel B., 24, 43, 46
Fickinger, John B., 27, 34, 91
Fidler, Henry, 18, 20, 24, 25
Finch, George H. 83, 84, 86
Finn, Robert W., 49
Forbes, Frank M., 79, 81
French, William H., 40, 91
Gibbons, John, 80
Gingrich, Henry, 50, 52
Gingrich, Mary, 3
Gorman, John, 21
Grant, William H., 40, 86
Gregg, John C., 56
Griswold, George G., 24, 85, 86
Hamilton, John R., 52
Hamlin, James H., 43, 85
Hancock, Winfield Scott, 14, 30, 65, 69, 80, 76
Harris, Mrs. John, 102
Harrison, N. L., 75, 76, 88
Hayes, William, 94
Hays, Harrison H., 80
Heintzelman, Samuel Peter, 70
Henry, Samuel, 84, 86, 87
Hilton, John C., 52, 80, 84
Hooker, Joseph, 57, 61, 65
Howard, Oliver O., 59, 110
Hubbard, John H., 44, 92
Jareski, Henry, 52
Jewett, George T., 89
Kearney, Philip A., 71
Keefer, Samuel W., 36
Ketchaus, Elizabeth, 19
King, David D., 46
Lewis, Horatio F., 76, 84, 86
Long, Daniel, 44
Loomis, Dyer, 13, 25, 29, 64
Loomis, George Lamertine, 13, 18
Lynch, Charles M., 36, 44, 93
Lyon, George A., 49
Mann, Horace, 83
Marker, Mrs. Perry, 96

139

Marsh, Joseph, 81
Mason, Andrew J., 44
Maury, Matthew Fontaine, 40, 41, 43, 46
McClellan, George B., 13, 16, 29, 97
McCreary, David Berkley, 14, 20, 33, 40, 46, 59, 69, 83, 93, 94, 95, 96, 98, 103
McCreary, Mrs. David Berkley, 52
Meade, George G., 76, 77, 90, 96, 98, 105
Meagher, Thomas Francis, 14, 17, 57
Mitchell, L. H., 65, 66, 76, 90, 98, 105
Mosby, John Singleton, 96, 97
Mowry, James S., 36
Nixdorff, George Augustus, 89
Oliver, Moses W., 64, 79, 92, 93
Olmstead, Miss S. L., 69
Parker, Ezra A., 18, 20, 26, 33, 36
Patton, John W., 5
Payne, James G., 103
Pierce, Bryon E., 43, 46
Pleasanton, Alfred, 98
Porter, Fitz John, 30
Potter, George L., 25, 30, 33, 34, 36, 41, 78, 102
Reynolds, Francis, 89
Reynolds, John Fulton, 76
Reynolds, John W., 40, 46, 69, 72, 75, 78, 81, 93, 96, 98, 101, 108, 109
Riblet, Charles H., 44
Richardson, Albert C., 21
Ruess, Frederick, 52, 68
Shelton, Andrew Flint, 103
Sigel, Franz, 71
Skinner, Henry, 51
Slocum, George W., 79, 80
Smart, George F. C., 64

Smith, William "Extra Billy," 98
Stallman, Lewis, 83
Startzman, Christian, 12
Sterrett, Edwin C., 34
Stevens, William Henry, 56, 62
Stewart, Hugh R., 64
Stiles, Kimball H., 36, 105
Stohlman, Karl Frederick Edward, 19
Stork, Theophilus, 75
Stover, Martin Luther, 87
Stultz, Martin L., 46, 52
Sumner, Edwin Vose, 37, 38, 59
Talmadge, H. L., 81
Taylor, J. Milton, 81
Thomas, Samuel, 19
Valandigham, Clemet L., 52
Vincent, John W., 44
Vincent, Strong, 5
Walker, John W., 11, 13, 16, 27, 48, 92
Walker, Mrs. John W., 48
Ward, Milton, 25, 26
Ware, Seymour D., 97
Warren, Gouverneur Kemble, 98
Weidler, Samuel B., 66
Welles, Gideon, 108
Whillden, J. S., 78, 94
Wicks, William D., 43
Williams, Erastus, 36
Williams, Levi T., 76
Wilson, Stacy, 28, 36, 56
Wise, Peter, 103
Wittich, James F., 17, 18, 20
Wittich, Mrs. James F., 28, 30
Wood, William W. W., 16, 17, 44, 47
Zook, Samuel, 78